MORNING ALTARS

MORNING ALTARS

A 7-Step Practice to Nourish Your Spirit through Nature, Art, and Ritual

Day Schildkret

The Countryman Press
A division of W. W. Norton & Company
Independent Publishers Since 1923

To Rudy Bear,
the little one who got me wandering
out on the land every morning
and is now resting within her.

CONTENTS

A NOTE FROM THE AUTHOR

During these tumultuous times, our humanity is slipping through our very fingers. So much that was once reliable is crumbling, and what has been long remembered is now being forgotten. Encountering the mythical and meaningful in nature, in community, in life purpose, in the everyday ways of living are disappearing as the glowing screens entrance and distract us from presence and connection. The breakneck speed of our days deceive us into thinking that busyness and productivity are the keys to a happy life. But without a practiced capacity to slow down and savor the subtleties, we are left ridden with anxiety, overwhelm, and exhaustion. Division and confusion pervade our collective conversations, and are reminders that we are living in a world ever more negligent toward and in real need of the fundamentals that make us human and healthy, the very threads that can tie us back together again.

Art, nature, and ritual have always offered a light in dark places. Individually, they can tether us to presence, purpose, and beauty during unpredictable times, rooting us into what truly matters and guiding a way back to our hearts and homes. Together they can serve as an antidote to some of the most challenging struggles we face both as a people and as a culture. They can help us practice creativity in the midst of disempowerment, to see with curiosity and wonder when so much looks like hopelessness and despair, and to exercise awareness and surrender through the transitory nature of life. These are real skills that we need in order to mend the tattered fabric of our humanity.

For hundreds of thousands of years, people all over the world have nourished life through ritualized earth art. From Stonehenge in England to the Giant Serpent Mound in Ohio to the Nazca Lines in Peru to the Chauvet Caves in France and to the totem poles of the Pacific Northwest Native Americans, the Earth has always served as a collaborator to express the myth, prayer, and memory of the people. Even for modern humans, the ritual of earth art can faithfully tie us back into a greater story of our small but significant place on this floating planet.

This book humbly and proudly stands on the shoulders of giants. As millions of people around the world continue to pass down their traditions of impermanent earth art, they remind us that while the art may not last, the ritual remains as cherished as ever. On a weekly basis, I get messages from people in India, Nepal, and Tibet who share with me generations of their family's customs of making earth altars in the form of rangolis, mandalas, kolams, alpanas, and muggus. I also receive messages from people in Peru and Vanuatu offering photos of their despachos and sandroings. Whether they are made from sand, volcanic ash, clay, rice or corn, these earth altars are woven into the fabric of the families and the cultures. They are beautiful and functional expressions of gratitude that serve to heal physical and emotional ailments, restore balance, honor births, grieve deaths, and provide offerings to the spirits of the land.

Even our Western culture has a relationship with ephemeral earth art through sandcastles, snow sculptures, jack-o'-lanterns, and Easter eggs. Interestingly, these playful nature expressions are almost all consigned to child's play while "serious" adult art is housed in museums and galleries. In the 1960s and '70s, in conjunction with greater environmental awareness, visionaries of the modern Land Art Movement paved a way for peo- ple of this Western culture to connect art and the natural world again. These efforts freed art from the confines of the museums, and the commodities markets, brought it outside and let the art belong to no one and everyone simultaneously. I would do well to honor visionaries such as Robert Smithson, Robert Long, Michael Heizer, Nancy Holt, Ana Mendieta, Cornelia Konrads, Dieter Voorwold, Mary Miss, and of course, Andy Goldsworthy.

Our modern culture tells us often, like a mantra, that bigger and faster are better. But as we face such peril that we have never encountered before on this Earth, within our communities and ourselves, I submit that a way through these troubled times can be found in beholding the ordinary and smallest of things. The fallen leaves or spiraling pinecone can tutor us in the needed skills of wonder and mystery, reawakening our imaginations as people who can behold magnificence. This book describes a landscape of enchantment. It not only strives to captivate you with the images of the altars but also weave you into a tangible practice and ritual that can connect you back to the pace of the Earth, channel your distractions, and offer you a way to bring meaning, mindfulness, and beauty to your life and to life itself in a time when it is truly needed.

As you wake up tomorrow morning, consider the question that Antonio Machado so eloquently asks:

What have you done with the garden that was entrusted to you?

February 2018

INTRODUCTION

We are debris arrangers. Equipped with what we have inherited, we try to make a life, make a living and make art. We are assemblers. We forge received parts into meaningful compositions. This state of affairs is our plight and our destiny, but it also offers the opportunity to find meaning as well as to find communion with others.

—*Anne Bogart, Theater Director*

Dawn has arrived. It's deeply quiet. Wildcat Canyon, the place I call home, is beginning to stir. And my broken heart aches. The year is 2014 and all I can do to find my footing after the most grief-soaked breakup of my life is to walk my dog in these Northern Californian hills. It calms my mind. Rudy, my fourteen-year-old miniature schnauzer, leads the way. We go slowly. Beauty envelops us as we trudge forward. As much as I try to avert my eyes, the land continues to present us with beautiful gifts that won't be denied: a leaf that somehow has managed to host all of the autumn colors, eucalyptus caps that look like an ancient temple tile from Morocco, and the sleek, jet-black tail wing feather of the neighborhood crow. I receive these gifts. They're balm for my tender heart.

Every morning after the breakup we would walk, wandering in sorrow, and every time we'd return home with some fallen land treasure. Eventually, I started bringing a basket on these walks because I'd discover so much beauty that it had to be collected. Focusing on the hunt got me out of my head. One early misty morning, Rudy and I came upon a village of amber mushrooms at the foot of a towering eucalyptus forest. I was enchanted. There was magic in the air that morning with the fog rolling through the hills and the sun barely having risen,

and these mushrooms, looking like they were painted with watercolor, roused me out of my heavy heart. I collected some and, to my dog's dismay, sat down for a while with the longing to create something beautiful.

I was no stranger to building art out of nature. When I was five years old, I would run outside after every rainstorm and witness the driveway covered in displaced and homeless worms, wiggling around trying to find their way back into the ground. I felt so much sympathy for the pathetic worms that I would dig small holes in the earth and escort the worms back into their proper place. But I didn't stop there. I wanted their little homecomings to be celebrated with beauty. So I would adorn each hole, creating miniature art installations with flower petals, tiny sticks, and fallen berries, until a constellation of wormhole mandalas scattered the front yard. I had fallen in love with this timeless expression—making beauty right outside my front door.

And so I sat with those mushrooms, wondering if crafting something beautiful could help ease my broken heart and soothe my agitated mind. I jumped in. Two wet hours later, I emerged from the otherworld of my imagination having created a piece of earth art I would later call *A Midnight Storm* (page 12). It was built out of those very mushrooms and the surrounding eucalyptus caps, bark, and buttons. I immediately felt lighter, like a heavy burden I'd been struggling to carry had been temporarily lifted. For the first time since the breakup I wasn't only suffering from my grief but found a way to express that grief creatively. As the sun peaked and the fog rolled, this beauty-making experience took me out of my woe-is-me mind and brought me into my hands and into the earth.

That moment inspired me to make a commitment that

eventually became a practice: to return to the base of the eucalyptus tree on the top of that hill overlooking the East Bay every morning for the next month and to create art out of nature. Before my mind could repeat its loop of regretful thinking, I grabbed a basket, a pair of scissors, and my dog and went out into the hills at dawn. I took the heartache I felt and employed it to make something beautiful each morning for a solid month. I felt like I was placing my grief on an altar and letting it go, which is how the name Morning Altars came into being. An altar's purpose is to sanctify something and offer it up to a higher source. And without even thinking about it, that's what I was doing with my grief.

After one month I realized I had no intention of stopping. My mornings were now richer than they ever had been, filled with curiosity, wonder, and blessings. I felt a far more intimate connection with the place where I lived. With my hands, I was making a new beautiful offering out of the land every day. My imagination was uncorked. What began as a way to be with my own heartache transformed into a faithful and creative resource and daily practice that made my life more meaningful.

The altars weren't just about grief. Over time, I made Morning Altars for every life event: to honor my friend giving birth to a baby girl, to process the decision to leave my job, or simply because I felt grateful for waking up that morning. And the altars started to have a life of their own, impacting people in ways I could never imagine. Beauty has a way of doing that. Sometimes, I would find "Thank you" or "I love this" spelled out in branches or acorns on public trails in the same spot I had built an altar the day before. The people and the Earth were speaking through one another.

Most significantly, this practice was weaving me and the place I called home into a deeply purposeful and generous relationship. I was belonging more to and becoming more of this place in ways I had never before. The altars bound my heart, hands, and home more closely together.

THE SEVEN MOVEMENTS FOR A MORNING ALTARS PRACTICE

** Note: These seven movements are just a guide. The most important thing is that you try!
Maybe one day you'll do them completely out of order or skip a few, and that's totally fine.
I do that all the time, so don't sweat it.*

1 Wander & Wonder: This is a treasure hunt that transforms the mundane into the magical as you forage the treasures that will fill your altar.

2 Place: Practice listening to the place that calls you. Sit on the earth and experience a "Place Meditation." Connect more deeply to where you are and witness the place come alive as it might have never before.

3 Clear: Use a brush or your hand to clear the space at your feet and reveal your blank canvas. It is an act that helps you clear space so that a new creative inspiration can flow in again.

4 Create: It's all play! Explore shapes and patterns as you learn the language of how to bring together many different pieces into one gorgeous work of art, which is what the universe is doing all the time.

5 Gift: Practice generosity. Learn to set an intention for your Morning Altar. Devote it as an offering for your life, as a celebration of your family's well-being, as a gift to your ancestors, or as a way to mark an occasion.

6 Share: Photograph and share your beauty making and intentions with your friends, community, or even with people you've never met.

7 Let Go: Practice walking away. Bearing witness to the impermanence of the art is an exercise that will strengthen your capacity for unattachment, grace, and change.

This book not only tells my personal story of how beauty making with the Earth has enlivened my day-to-day life, but it also describes the innumerable ways this practice has helped me belong to something greater than myself. Over the years, while cultivating this devotional and daily Morning Altars practice, I have discovered seven movements within this art form. Each movement elevates the art from a creative expression to a ritual. These seven movements offer a tangible, interactive way to get you outside and cause you to immediately relate to the greater-than-human world through a sense of wonder, play, and reverence. I have taught this to thousands of people, and I've come to witness how simple and yet profound this practice is. It is accessible to anyone, anywhere, at any age. I see this book as a resource that can ignite a global movement, inspiring earth altars to pop up like temporary and tiny universes in landscapes all over the world, reminding us of our enduring connection to the Earth and each other.

Chapter 1 contains the first movement and is devoted to the dying art of wandering. It will inspire you to step out of your front door, leave behind what you think is the right way, and let your childlike sense of curiosity guide you onward. It invites you to step off your familiar way and introduces you into what author Robert MacFarlane calls "the language of landscape." This chapter's goal is to enliven your eyes and whet your imagination so that the twisted knot in a branch or the pop of pink in a berry enraptures you, as you fill your basket with the treasures you discover along the way.

In Chapters 2 through 7, I will share the step-by-step process of arriving to the place where you will sit and build your Morning Altar. I will guide you through meaningful ways of connecting to that place, clearing a circle of earth as a way of clearing your mind, creating from your center, and then letting it all go. Each movement is a hands-on practice that will not just address how to build a Morning Altar, but also why this simple, elegant practice is so needed in this day and age.

Throughout the book, I refer to places, trees, plants, and the Earth in general through the feminine pronouns of "her" and "she" instead of the words "it" or "that." I do this in a conscious effort to subjectify, not objectify, nature. My hope is that this book will serve to bring you into a closer relationship with the phenomenal animate world. One of the ways I choose to do that is by anthropomorphizing all things Earth. It is similar to the idea put forward by linguist Benjamin Lee Whorf: that the language we learn and use shapes the universe we can imagine.

This book concludes with heartfelt stories and photos from people all over the world who have been inspired to try their hands at creating a Morning Altar. From honoring a parent's death, revisiting a childhood home, or dealing with the stress of politics, these stories represent a global movement of people who are utilizing earth art to make their lives more meaningful, beautiful, and purposeful.

Morning Altars is like a cookbook filled with a visual feast meant to inspire you to nourish your life. It is my hope that the stories move you, the wisdom empowers you, and that the seven-step recipe teaches you how to craft your own beautiful earth altars to not just feed your life but as an offering back to this wild and wonderful planet.

Chapter 1

WANDER & WONDER

All that is gold does not glitter,
Not all those who wander are lost.

—*J. R. R. Tolkien*

A Treasure Hunt

Treasure is hidden all over your neighborhood. Most people can't see it. Perhaps even you, at times, have missed it. What makes this treasure so inconspicuous is that it simply appears in the place you live: berries, leaves, pinecones. The stuff you walk on, or walk past, because you're busy or distracted and have seen it ten thousand times. But look again. Look at that leaf—the confluence of veins is like many rivers coming together. Notice the spiraling geometric pattern on that golden pinecone. Gaze into the aged bark peeling away like parchment paper. Examine the delicate cloud of puff perched atop that dandelion flower.

There is a wealth of beauty and wonder littered all around us, right outside our own front door. We have just forgotten how to see it. To paraphrase Marcel Proust, "The real voyage of discovery consists not in seeking new lands but seeing with new eyes." This chapter is meant to give you these new eyes. The kind you once had when you were younger, when days lasted forever and the world was alive and enchanting. That way of seeing was so effortless back then. You could spend hours playing in the sand, chasing fireflies, or watching the tireless journey of a single ant. The small and common were doorways into an entire universe where everything was a playground. Distraction was an asset outdoors that brought you to the next more interesting thing. Once upon a time, we all had access to this way of seeing. But like a muscle, when we don't employ a sense of wonder and curiosity at the living world around us, it fades away. Then the world we look at is shaped through the lens of what we expect to see, which itself is a fraction of what there is to behold.

> The feeling of awe and sense of wonder arises from the recognition of the deep mystery that surrounds us everywhere, and this feeling deepens as our knowledge grows.
>
> —*Anagarika Govinda*

Wonder

Step one of this practice is the foraging for your materials, the gathering of your palette of colors, textures, and shapes that will inspire the brilliance of your Morning Altar. But you are not just collecting things to make art—you are exercising a skill: your capacity to be enamored by the ordinary and to behold the insignificant. A single blade of grass, for instance, can be the needed element to inspire your creation. You must focus the lens of curiosity. Practice looking more closely: How is the grass shaped? Is the top flat or pointed? What is this shade of green? Is the browning tip causing a faded ombré effect? This kind of attentiveness toward the looked-over is how we truly discover our relationship to the place where we are. As the poet David Whyte says, our "alertness is the hidden discipline of familiarity."

Not too long ago, I was sitting in a teepee around a fire late into the night at Stephen Jenkinson's farm in Ontario, Canada. Stephen is the founder and teacher of the Orphan Wisdom School, a teaching and learning house of the skills of deep living and making of human culture. My gaze was torn between the flickering beauty of the bright warm fire we were gathered around and the glory of that nighttime celestial ceiling, which was glittering with starlight seen through the small hole in the top of the teepee. Both of those sights brought me into a profound sense of peace and awe at the ancientness of life. With perfect timing, I heard Stephen say, almost as if he was reading my mind: "Wonder takes a willingness to be uncertain." There was silence after a statement like that.

What he was asking from those of us gathered around the fire was to consider a willingness to let loose our tight grasp on how we think things should be, our preferences and opinions, and lean into the greater mysteries that we are woven into. Perhaps wondering about mysterious things is more accessible out on a farm during a vast and timeless night. But the real practice is to take that wondering home and be willing to marvel at the mundane in our everyday. Rabbi Abraham Joshua Heschel calls this "radical amazement." For instance, the miracle of simply waking up in the morning really deserves a lot more interest than most of us probably give it. Imagine being radically amazed at the utter miracle of opening your eyes every morning. What if we refuse to get used to the common subtleties of life and instead invite ourselves to engage them as small splendors?

Honestly, doing this is not easy. One of the great obstacles of this first movement—the saboteur that will attempt to prevent you from discovering the natural hidden treasures in your neighborhood—is your certainty, a sense that you already know how things are. Certainty is that defended mindset that has convinced you that there's nothing more to be learned because you've got it figured out already. Certainty is the anesthetic of wonder and is unutterably uninterested in that which is already contained in its storehouse of knowledge. The only way to break through that well-fortified wall of surety is to reconsider and look again. The movements and changes in nature are constant, and although your mind may be convinced that it knows exactly what you're seeing, step closer and look again. Look at the detail and try saying something like: "Wow! What are you?" This may sound silly, but it initiates wondering. Certainty lets you keep your distance, but wondering is a courtship that draws you closer. It whispers, "Isn't existence just miraculous?"

Less Expectation, More Fascination

Once I was building a large-scale Morning Altar for a popular music festival in California. It was summertime and we were in the midst of a drought, so much so that the land was hard and dry. When I first got to the site, I wandered about scouting for flowers, plants, or anything with color that wasn't brown or green. I went for a long wander and looked for hours but couldn't find anything that inspired me. My mind was made up that the color palette of this place and of this piece would be limited to two dull colors. Certainty had set its stubborn little roots down in my mind. But then I remembered: *Look again.* And I did. I let my eyes wander. Hidden in a bit of dusty earth I saw what looked like a pearl-size turquoise stone. I stepped closer, picked it up, and asked, "What are you?" It looked like a micro Earth, with black, cracked continents filled with a gorgeous,

turquoise ocean. But here's the thing, and I kid you not: My curiosity had me comb my hands in the earth, and to my fascination I discovered thousands more turquoise stones loosely buried under the surface in that very spot. "Where did you come from?" "How long have you been here?" I was out in the wilderness and out of all the places I could have looked, I had been drawn to that one particular spot. Why? I couldn't say. And I still can't. It is a great unsolvable mystery, the kind that outlives any attempt to answer it.

If wondering is a dance, then questions are its choreography. Good questions move you. They connect you to that which you're wondering about. And the purpose of asking questions is not so you can finish dancing but so you can get more into the dance. Questions woo you out of yourself, out of the rigidity and isolation of your mind, and bring you into deeper connection with all of life that dances with you. When you wonder, you should resist asking utilitarian questions that try to solve the mystery. You are not mining for answers. This is a beauty-making practice, and it begins long before you sit down to make an altar. Craft a beautiful question. Let it roam wild in the space of your consideration. Have it carry some humbleness, some awe, and a willingness to listen. Speak *with* that which you are wondering about, not *about* it. Wondering, like dancing, is a conversation that moves back and forth. Maybe that flower in your hand is also wondering about you too.

A WONDERING EXERCISE

Step outside.

See a fallen leaf.

Before you go toward it, approach with
curiosity. Did its color catch your eye?

Does its shape attract you?

Where did it come from?

To what tree does it belong to?

Exercise your fascination.

Pick it up and hold it in your hand
and ask: What are you?

Pause and listen.

How is it communicating to you?

Through detail? Describe it.

Through color? Describe it.

Through texture? Describe it.

In what ways does it inspire you?

Does it want to collaborate with you?

Take a moment.

Imagine making more beauty with it.

This is your first treasure.

Wander

Step One's next practice is the anti-spiritual wisdom. Rather than seeking to find a path, I advise you to go off it. Don't walk in straight lines. Get distracted. Take the long way. Roam! Wander! Explore! Let the scent of a warm, fragrant breeze tempt you in a completely new direction. Follow that spritely sparrow under the shrub. Get out of your head, get out of your home, and put that wondering mind in some wandering shoes. Open your front door and *be taken, be taken, be taken.*

If you can believe it, I once lived on a grid. While I currently reside inside Wildcat Canyon in Northern California (and went to high school in Florida), I am a born and raised New Yawka. And for almost ten years I lived not just in New York City, but in Times Square. Every hour thousands of people would pass by my front door, walking at a pace that some would call a slow jog. During this time of my life, while working on and off Broadway, I wanted to be part of it all. I wanted to live near the theater district, surrounded by skyscrapers and flashing lights and people who spoke a mile a minute. I loved the direction and pace. Everyone knew where they were going: rushing to the subway, running to work, or racing to a show. It was exhilarating.

I remember one day dashing to the nearest subway, late as usual, only to discover it was closed. Having to take an alternative route, I passed by a community garden that I had never noticed. It was a rarity to find a green oasis in the middle of Times Square. The scent of it reached me first: roses and that spicy sweet tang of jasmine. I slowed, a bit intoxicated. Over the wrought iron fence, I saw a blossoming magnolia tree. Its falling white and lavender petals littered the sidewalk. I stopped—enchanted. It felt more like springtime in Paris than New York. Peering in from the street, I saw a stark contrast to the city: a flourish of floral delight, chirping birds, and people lounging in the grass and dozing in the warm spring sun. Just the sight of this secret garden had the power to unwind and open me. And right in my own neighborhood, nonetheless! Someone was leaving and held the gate. There was a certain kind of courtship at play and I was being invited inside. I grabbed the gate, my curiosity getting the better of me. But then I let the gate go while still standing on the outside. I had somewhere to be and declined the invitation to deviate—I refused the wander.

But something shifted that day, like removing a small stone that unsettles the entire foundation of a house. I realized that I was destination addicted. That day I realized the cost: I didn't really know my own neighborhood. That garden was only two blocks from my home, but to me it had never existed. I had always taken the same streets to the subway and rarely diverged from them. I wondered what else I was missing by walking so quickly and in such straight and determined lines.

The path of freedom has no markers, yet leads to fulfillment; the path of confusion is crowded with signs, pointing in all directions. The Great Way is a humble, solitary path leading home; follow it closely and be guided. How do you know you are on the way? When your map no longer serves you.

—Haven Trevino

The Four Big Worries of Wandering

Wandering is not easy to do in our modern lives. With our jammed-packed calendars, overwhelmed workloads, family responsibilities, and daily routines, it's enormously challenging to find the time to let ourselves go off track. Even more so, even if we had more time, certain fears might surface that prevent us from wandering. At a recent workshop, I asked the group to name some fears and worries that would stop them from wandering. They responded:

"I'll get lost."

"I won't get to where I should go."

"I won't find what I'm looking for."

"I won't get there on time."

Yes, all of these worries may come true. But leaving behind the path doesn't mean you are lost. Lost means that something is gone, but wandering means something else entirely. Wandering is the practiced art of listening and letting yourself be drawn to that which is here, alive, and communicating. Wandering is not aimless—it's attentive. You're not gone, you are truly arriving. It requires you to become attuned to where you are by observing what else is there with you: to the handsome crow cawing above you, to the warm, western breeze at the back of your neck, or to the tree in the park with the knotted trunk that looks like an old person's face. Wandering asks you to step out of self-direction and efficiency. It asks you to give up the ways you think you should go, an obsession that plagues us in this culture, and enter into a roaming relationship with the rest of life.

People and animals have been wandering since the beginning of time. If you look back far enough, you will

LEAVE ⅔ RULE

For the most part, I prefer to create altars out of plants that have fallen to the ground. I love the idea of resurrecting something that a tree or animal has let go of naturally and then give it another life by making art with it. Yet, there are times when I do cut a leaf or a flower because I am inspired by its beauty and can imagine it as the perfect component to fulfill the vision of the altar.

Yet, in these moments I have a "Leave ⅔ Rule."

If I see a patch of wild daisies, for instance, I will only harvest no more than ⅓ of what is there and leave ⅔. This rule provides boundaries that prevent me from taking too much, and it reminds me to forage lightly and sparingly.

The "Leave ⅔ Rule" serves as a great reminder that these plants are not just here for my taking and that, like any relationship, we must not show up always looking to take whatever we want. Sometimes less is more, and minimizing our impact helps to maintain the health of the plant.

find that every single culture is founded on a nomadic past. All people once migrated with the seasons, with the animals, with the rains—with all the movements of the land. The land spoke to the people and the people listened and moved with her. That movement is evident in the word itself. The etymological origin of *wander* comes from the old Proto-Indo-European word *wendh* meaning to weave, wind, or turn. There's an elegant back and forth movement in the very root of this word.

Like weaving, over time these migratory movements created patterns. And these patterns had purpose. What looked like an aimless homelessness was actually the land weaving the people into a very expansive understanding of what it means to be at home.

Leaving your home is really the first ritual of your Morning Altar practice. It is also a potential saboteur that can prevent you from actually doing it. Taking that first step out of the house means leaving behind the familiar. It means giving up the warmth of your bed and the comfort of things placed how you like them. It means overcoming fear and beginning the journey toward something unknown. The modern choreographer Twyla Tharp says that it is the ritual of getting in the cab every morning to go to her dance studio that is vital for the success of her creative process. It is the very first simple and powerful step of crossing a threshold. It's like what the character Bilbo Baggins says in *The Lord of the Rings,* "It's a dangerous business, Frodo, going out your front door. You step onto the road, and if you don't mind your feet, there's no knowing where you might be swept off to."

What I've come to understand is that when I leave my front door to go wander and forage, I am leaving my house but I am not actually leaving my home. I am

being invited to consider a broader understanding of what it means to be home, which is not defined by walls or an address but includes all those that call that place home too: the hills, the many streets and front yards, the deer, the canyon, the city, the hummingbirds, the beach, the redwoods, the creek. In this more spacious home, I begin to remember where others live. "Oh, I remember where that bush with the red berries is." Listening and wandering is our ancestral technology that never lets us be disconnected because we are being claimed by the place itself.

Foraging

The treasure hunt is ready to begin, but please read this brief note before you set off on your journey:

When you wander, bow your head.

I mean this both practically and spiritually.

Practically speaking, look for the gifts that have fallen. While I sometimes pluck, cut, and tear, my preference is always to forage for that which has already given itself. Look down and see the beauty littered at your feet.

Bow your head also means to wander humbly.

You are receiving gifts from the land. Please do not just take them. Give first. The industrial, consumer world we were born into has helped us forget how to be gracious. There's a certain sense of entitlement that runs rampant

THE BASICS:
Wandering

A large basket or bag for big treasures
A few smaller bags for those delicate items
A pair of scissors
Water and a snack
A timer*
A willingness to be awed by the ordinary

Note: Wandering is a timeless endeavor, but it shouldn't last forever. Set a time of when you want to be called back home. My suggestion is to wander and forage for anywhere between 30 minutes to an hour and a half. If you have all day, go for it!

these days, and it is severely damaging to our generous Earth. Let this first step be a practice that directly opposes that.

When I forage and find something for the altar, I give something before taking: a thank you, a song, a sigh. Something for the land. I see myself as a guest, and as a guest there's a certain kind of courtesy that is required when I visit. Remember: This entire practice, not just the fourth step of creating, is a beauty-bringing endeavor. Let your graciousness overflow with beauty as well.

Chapter 2

PLACE

If what a tree or a bush does is lost on you,
You are surely lost. Stand still. The forest knows
Where you are. You must let it find you.

—*David Wagoner*

A Place

So here we are. You've come back from your destination-less wander, you've collected your horde of neighborhood treasure, and now you're ready to find a spot and start creating.

Not so fast.

There's one last treasure to find. You've walked all around it but have yet to truly discover it. Maybe it's located high in the piñon pine and perched atop those sticky sap-filled branches, or perhaps its underneath that gnarly grand oak, hidden in the same spot the squirrels hide their acorns. This last treasure is elusive, but if you keep wandering about you may never really find it. There's something else entirely that you must do to let this one find you. It doesn't require any more wandering. Actually, there's nowhere else to go. You've got to plant yourself somewhere to discover it. You've got to get quiet and let it come to you. Could it be that you are so close to it that you're already seeing it right now? Perhaps it's already there—or here?

The treasure *is* here, all around you. This beautiful, mundane, epic, familiar, grassy, rocky, urban, suburban, beachy, dusty, mossy, wooded place you find yourself is the remaining treasure. Wherever that is, wherever you are, here it is.

Take it in and be taken in by it. Let yourself arrive as the place comes to meet you.

But this isn't just a "Hey, how are you?" kind of arrival. That's the sort of quasi-greeting with one foot in and one foot out the door—you're here but already on to the next thing. Instead, can you let yourself really and truly arrive? Sit down for a while so you can learn the particular ways this place expresses herself in the world—how she moves, sings, smells. Notice which trees live here, which birds call this place home, the direction the wind blows, the trajectory of the sun, and the way the shadows are cast. After some time of trying to learn this place, she may even begin to share secrets with you that you would never have discovered had you just walked past her or stayed indoors. Over time, you may even begin to feel that you are in a relationship with her, one that might even spark an outright love affair. You should only be so lucky!

But first things first. Come with the gift of your presence and attention. These are the necessary ingredients for this relationship and, honestly, for any relationship. Your attentiveness tells whomever you're with that you are willing to look beyond yourself and really learn who you're with. So much of the time, in all too many relationships, we stop tending that fire of curiosity and generosity because we think we already know who we're with or where we are. We let the "I know" become a spell of familiarity that prevents us from staying engaged, enlivened, and interested. Our certainty eventually becomes disinterest. Then we start looking elsewhere, which is the consequence of not fully connecting to and staying curious with all that is here.

So let's begin the dance of learning about the place where we are. It's what I call "the courtship of here." And let's see if that place is moved to meet you. Only then can you be on your way to creating your Morning Altar.

When we approach [things]
with reverence, great things
decide to approach us.

—*John O'Donohue*

The Approach:
A Love Story

There was once a tree that I would have liked to live with for a thousand years. Her home is near the Ho'opi'i Falls on the island of Kauai in Hawaii. I was on vacation and hiking the trail when I first saw her from a distance. I almost walked by because there's something about being on a path that compels you to just keep moving forward. But the swift and immediate downpour of tropical rain forced me to scamper up the hill for some dry ground.

As I approached the circle where the tree stood, the first thing that caught my eye was her dress. Full and elegant, her branches drooped low like a hoop skirt, the kind that ripples out forever like a pebble in a pond. The floor around her was littered with the softest faded carpet of last year's leaves. The rain fell harder and I found my way closer. I wanted shelter but there was something else entirely that was pulling me in. I discovered her doorway, but in order to enter I had to bow below her branches. It was akin to entering into a teepee, where the etiquette is built into the architecture.

Immediately, I knew my approach to her mattered. When I bowed my head and entered beneath the tree, it reminded me of the ways I've entered into synagogues, mosques, and churches, with a sense of respect. And so I shut off my phone, shushed the voices in my head, and heightened my awareness, because I was reorienting to what felt like holy ground.

An approach is the way you draw close. It is the precursor to coming together with another and informs the way you actually do so. The approach itself carries with it and expresses all the ways you care or don't care about that which you are approaching.

I like to think of an approach as the choreography of orientation. You understand *what* you come to by *the way* you come to it. A neighbor near my home is a botanist, and we connect about plants and trees all the time because we both love them. As a scientist, when he looks at plants, he sees names, objects, measurements, studies, and information. But from what I can tell, it's rare that he lets himself be in an experience deeper than the data. So that is how the place manifests itself to him: He approaches as a scientific observer and he is met with a world of names and numbers.

In the book *Braiding Sweetgrass,* author and botanist Robin Wall Kimmerer tells the story of a plant scientist who goes into the rainforest to search for new botanical discoveries and hires a young indigenous guide for the journey. Along the way, the young guide points to and names many rare and unusual species, knowing how interested the scientist is to learn about these plants. This knowledge actually surprises the scientist. "Well, well, young man, you certainly know the names of a lot of these plants." The young guide responds by saying, "Yes, I have learned the names of all the bushes, but I have yet to learn their songs."

My approach to that tree in Hawaii carried reverence. Therefore, what greeted me inside was reverent. I sat down within her green inner sanctuary, her dark womb, as the rains fell and time seemed to stop. The forest had so much movement and such stillness at once. I looked up and noticed I wasn't alone. Two large white birds occupied her branches, probably wondering who the squatter was. I looked down and saw a line of ants marching in a winding path, hauling their food and eggs out of the rain and into the dry shelter. Because my approach to this place was filled with authentic and generous curiosity, I was able to notice so much of the life that appeared above, below, and all around me.

On that magical and wet day in Hawaii near the Ho'opi'i Falls, it seemed that the heart of our courtship emerged through generosity. By giving my full, undivided attention, my rapped watchfulness and deep listening, I drew closer to the place and she drew closer to me. This courtship was asking me to slow down and settle in so that I could really listen to where I was and who I was in the presence of. "Listening in wild places," says Kimmerer, "we are audience to conversations in a language not our own." Perhaps true courtship is found in our willingness to learn another's language and to speak it back to them.

When you come to nature, it is your willingness to witness and listen that nourishes the place. Putting your phone away, pocketing your timepiece, and quieting your mind is what allows you to relax, listen to the symphony of the space, and learn all her many notes and chords sung by her chorus of buzzing, flying, swaying, standing, flowing, flapping beings. This is your gift of attention. And here's the thing about good courting—deep down it is reciprocal. I have been to theatrical productions where the audience offered such a divine attention to the actors that the actors, in return, gave a divine performance to the audience as a response to this attention. All night long we kept passing that gift back and forth. It was electric.

This electricity can run through our Morning Altars practice too. During this second movement, the more attention you gift, the more alive the place becomes, and back and forth and so on and so on.

Giving attention is a well-practiced craft. You can become more skillful at it the more you do it. Jon Young, the tracker and founder of the Wilderness Awareness School, teaches his students to find a daily "sit spot." This concept is very much in sync with the second movement of your Morning Altars practice. Young teaches his students to find a spot in nature to sit in every day and observe. This exercise is meant to grow and strengthen the cords of connection between the person and the place. It is meant to build a relationship, which develops through a commitment to show up, sit down, and listen. The consequence is that the more you claim a place, the more you are claimed by the place.

There are some places in the world that I sit with often and regularly, like the spot next to the edge of Wildcat Creek where the wild ferns grow. Other places, like underneath that majestic tree on Kauai, I have only visited once. Regardless, I practice bringing my full, loving, enormous attention as the gift I give. This is how I show respect and care. This is how I learn where I am. And this is how I attempt to learn the language of the place, a language that I can only begin to name as love.

A Game: Where Am I?

I once spent an entire summer building invisible art in a forest.

You heard me right. Invisible.

Or, more precisely, hidden.

It was 2004 and I was the artist in residence at a retreat center in upstate New York. My medium was everything that particular place provided: boulders, feathers, bark, and last season's dried and devoured ghost-leaves that I hung in patterns above, below, and around the forest's path. It all blended so beautifully into the fabric of the forest that it was too easy to miss. And most did.

Of the hundreds of people who visited the forest that summer, some especially to see the installations, about 80 percent saw no art. Nothing at all. They came, they walked, they left, and they wondered where it all was. But the 20 percent who discovered something unusual past the trees, or overhead stopped in their tracks, sensing they were on to something. Eyes squinting, head cocking, slowly turning until, voila!, "There it is." When they discovered a ceiling of dried leaves that resembled stained glass as the light poured through it, or a tree trunk wrapped in bright red feathers that offered the appearance of an otherworldly ball gown, some let out sounds like, "Oh!" or "Wow!" Most of them spent the rest of their walk through the forest somewhat altered. I guess they thought that if they found one, there was probably more to be found. Their walk became a game of hide-and-seek, and anywhere and everywhere became a potential hiding spot for the revelation of magic

and beauty. They were being courted into playing a game, and it changed the way they walked, talked, and listened because they now were sparked with a child-like curiosity and engagement. The entire forest came alive, and so did the people. The people and the forest were engaging each other. Those who were chatty walkers became unbelievably quiet and attentive; those who were distracted on their cellphones forgot about them entirely; and those who were fast walkers,

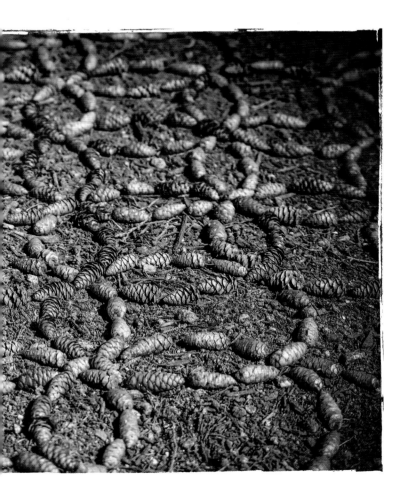

FORGET YOU KNOW WHERE YOU ARE AND ASK THE PLACE, "WHERE AM I?"

Asking a question like that has the potential to unsettle you, pull you in, and make you listen up. It challenges you to sidestep what you think you know about a place, all the ways you're familiar with it, and learn where you are from the place herself. You might even unlearn the name you call it.

Usually when we ask this question, "Where am I?" it is because we are looking for an answer. But, with our game, I am asking you to keep the question alive. Don't try to figure it out. Don't settle for a name or an answer. Let the place reveal her "whereness" to you. Feel into the "whereness" under your bum. Track the "whereness" by how the clouds are forming in the sky. Let her come to you with a response that sounds a lot like, "Here." Where am I? Here I am.

Observe.

the kind who zooms through places and doesn't pay much attention to where they are, rubbernecked the rest of the way. Those 20 percent let their senses guide them, and were "ooh-ing" and "wow-ing" not just at my art but at pieces created entirely by the forest herself. Nothing was exempt from magic. Everything became art. And what started as a very insular experience for some erupted into a very interactive one with the place. Their approach toward the forest changed

and, as a consequence, they were met with a forest full of wonder.

Once, I was teaching this very exercise of asking "Where am I?" when a tree fell in the forest. It was dramatic. We all heard the wind, then the snapping cracks, and then the whistling down. And, boom! The branches smacked the earth, the surrounding birds flew away, and we were left with silence. She spoke, letting us know where we were. It was something truly remarkable to experience.

But, more often than not, when you play this game trees won't fall, lightning won't crash, and a bald eagle won't fly over your head. Most likely, you will be practicing with what you consider to be familiar, like your backyard or local park. Familiar places might be the best places to play this game, at least at first, because the point of the game isn't to hear some epic blast that shouts, "You are here!" The point of this game isn't to capture the moment on your phone and post it on Instagram. Rather, the potent point of the game is to break the spell of the known and to practice opening yourself to the changing, mysterious, and nuanced ways of a place. It is to practice being enamored by the ordinary.

Keep asking that question or conjure your own. Let yourself wonder into the mystery of the place you're in and let the mystery wonder back at you.

Place Remembering

. . . what nature creates has eternity in it.

—*Isaac Bashevis Singer*

A place is a storyteller. The absolute best kind. Any storyteller who's worth a dime learned everything they know from a place. Just sitting with a place can enchant you into a timeless tale of the story of what went on there. If you allow her, a place will weave your own small story into a much bigger one. A place will tell you the story of the bioregion and the waterways. She will talk to you through animal tracks and bird songs, and the ways the creatures move over her and which ones in particular. She will tell you of how the landscape has changed over time and how it's changing right now. As you can imag-

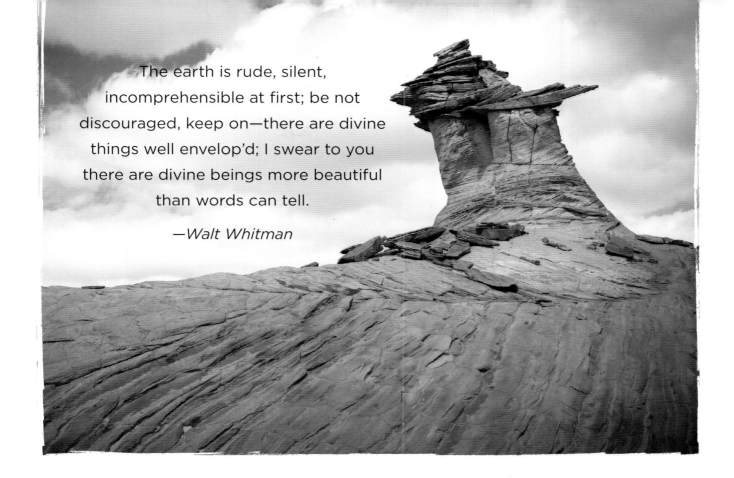

The earth is rude, silent, incomprehensible at first; be not discouraged, keep on—there are divine things well envelop'd; I swear to you there are divine beings more beautiful than words can tell.

—*Walt Whitman*

ine, there is an inexhaustible amount of stories to hear, if you're willing to listen.

A place is also a memory keeper. Each place does not just tell stories of what's happening now but also stories of what happened millions and millions of years ago. It was once, and in many places still is, understood that the people's stories emerged from the land herself, and the actual terrain of a particular place is where these stories are held and inform how they are transmitted. The rocky hills, rabbit holes, river's bend, vol-

cano's mouth, coyote's path, red sandy dunes, bottom of the lake, and salmon run are both the set and setting where the old stories occur and the actual place where the ancestral wisdom is embedded. The land remembers and the people remember through the land. As author David Abram says, "The animate, expressive terrain itself is the necessary mnemonic, or memory trigger, for remembering the oral tales." It is a living, symbiotic relationship of memory.

Recently, I had the opportunity to learn about the place

where I was living while writing much of this book. My companion was the man who is its current steward, Ron Johnson. Ron is doing incredible work to bring back the beavers that in turn, are rehabilitating the waterways that feed all of the natural habitat. He told me another fact, the one that continues to blow my mind: In this area, you can see evidence of what it was during the Paleozoic, Early and Late Jurassic, and Late Cretaceous periods. In sum, this would be between 543 and 65 million years ago. During the Paleozoic Era, Utah was at the western edge of North America and half of the state was covered by shallow inland seas. As the Early Jurassic period began, desert sands were forming dunes that have now become Navajo Sandstone. At the very spot where I am writing these sentences, during the Late Jurassic and Cretaceous periods, this place was a peninsula. Brachiosaurus, Stegosaurus, and even Utahraptors roamed here. And this land was the main highway for dinosaurs traveling up and down the continent when, according to the Utah Geological Survey, "The eastern portion of the state was covered by an inland sea that stretched from the Gulf of Mexico to the Arctic." The very landscape here remembers that time.

Not too far from the ranch where I am, there are other living memories in the land that tell the story of who else lived here. Anasazi or Ancestral Puebloan pictographs carved into the red rock tell the stories and ways that these people lived here between AD 1 and 1300. Some of their earthen structures, stone tools, and pottery are scattered throughout the land telling the story of where they lived, what they hunted, and how they sustained themselves. While hiking, I came across a small adobe container made of mud and sticks from at least nine hundred years ago that was most probably used for food storage. Being here in Boulder Mountain, Utah, reminds me that I am walking in a memory place.

When you sit wherever you are, can you ask yourself, "Who else sat here?" Consider what this place might have looked like hundreds, thousands, even millions of years before you came to sit there. Who else wandered that land? Who else was born and died there? Imagine what this place will look like hundreds, if not thousands of years beyond your life. Could it be that *that* hillside will still be here, witnessing the sun come and go as it has for millions of years?

The land lets us wonder into a time beyond our own.

It's incredibly humbling to put our lives into this much broader perspective, of which the land offers as a gift. Through our willingness to just slow down and sit with the land, listen and learn the ways to read her signs, it is possible to step out of our busy, distracted, incredibly self-centered lives and to step into something profound and mysterious. Our curiosity can open us up to the living Internet of the land that is uploading and downloading memory onto an eternal hard drive that tells the story of time.

Being a Guest

According to my elder and Shoshonne tribesman, Clyde Hall of Idaho, the Shoshonne people have been on their land for more than nine thousand years. Nine *thousand*. That amount of time shared between a people and a place is unfathomable to me.

Clyde says that to be indigenous is to be of the land. This means that over time you become part of the land and the land becomes part of you. There are so many generations in the ground that his people's bones literally make up the bones of the place. There is barely a distinction between place and people—they belong to each other. The people's language is informed by the landscape; the patterns of the place are sewn into the garments and the people's sacred foods are the berries, meat, water, blood, and corn from the land. Their oral mythology even speaks of the people being born from the very place itself. Clyde says that when a people have been someplace for so long, they carry a different understanding of home. They know home in a way that informs their entire culture.

During our conversation, Clyde asked me to consider wondering about those of us, myself included, who don't know home in this way. That consideration troubled me. As much as I love the place where I live, my family doesn't come from that place. In fact, we come from many places. He suggested there was a significant distinction between people who have lived in a place for thousands of years and someone who has lived in a place for fifty years. There is a different relationship formed with the land and, therefore, a different way of relating. Clyde referred to people who don't know home in this way as "permanent guests" and that such people have trouble understanding this concept of home because they move around so fast.

After speaking with him, I wondered about what it took to learn the skill of becoming a well-practiced guest—to slow down and understand the etiquette, conduct, and language of the place that hosts me—and what consequence that would bring to my relationship with the land.

All of us have been a guest at some point and have hosted a guest. Based on your experience, you can immediately tell the difference between a guest who is skillful, generous, and self-aware and one who isn't.

When you're in the presence of a well-practiced guest, you know it. They lend themselves to understanding the ways of the place they are visiting. Whenever I travel, I do my best to learn the basic courtesies and expressions of the town or country I visit: how to greet, to thank, to compliment, to say goodbye. Interestingly enough, the root sense of the word *guest*, which is from the Proto-Indo European word *ghos-ti*, refers to someone who has reciprocal duties of hospitality. What that means is that guests, like their hosts, have an obligation to be generous, inviting, and grateful.

Allowing a good long arrival is the hidden discipline of hospitality. It gives you and the land the space to draw closely to each other. Your way of coming to her, the "how" of how you come together, is the courtship in action. The alchemy of that way is found in the slowing down with each other. It is an act of recognition and welcoming. It obligates you to each other. To obligate doesn't mean that you are forced together, like most people think. More precisely it means to be temporarily bound together, in the way ligaments temporarily bind bones until death. When we take the time to come together slowly, gracefully, carefully, and beautifully, then the threads of our connection tie us into a relationship. It is the warp and weft weaving of hospitality.

To arrive is your sacred duty as a guest of the place.

A PLACE MEDITATION

SET A TIMER OR JUST GO FOR AS LONG AS YOU WANT.

Take your seat.
Just let your body meet the earth.
Feel the weight and gravity pulling you closely to her.
Perhaps even imagine that you have roots emerging
   from your tailbone,
and they begin to descend into the deep dark soil.

Let your skin take this place in.
Notice the temperature on your arms.
Notice if there is any breeze upon your face.
Is the sunlight bringing heat to your body?

Let your ears take this place in.
Do you hear the wind rustling the trees,
or the buzzing of any insects,
or perhaps the sound of a distant dog bark,
or humans speaking?

Let your nose take in this place.
Feel the air enter your nostrils.
What does this place smell like?
Do the trees give off their spicy scent?
Does the ocean have a particular smell?
Or maybe you are in a place that also carries
   the scent of human-made machines.
Where does this smell transport you to?

Let your eyes take in this place and zoom wide.
Soften your gaze and take in the entire place.
The contours of her landscape,
the colors that appear in your gaze,
the shadows dancing all around you,
the place where the sky meets the earth.
What is moving?
What stays still?
Do you see anyone watching you?

Let your eyes take in the place and get focused.
Narrow your gaze and focus on one thing.
Maybe it's the texture of the bark right in front of you,
or one single blade of grass recently cut.
Let your eyes notice all the details.
The color of that particular thing.
Its shape and movement.
How unique and utterly itself it is.

Spend one more moment
beholding this place.
Let it change before you,
witness the light come and go.

Consider how long this place has looked the way it does.
Who else was here yesterday
or last year
or 100 years ago
or 10,000 years ago
or 10 million years ago?
Let yourself wonder what this place may be after you
   leave it.

Once again, feel yourself sitting in this spot,
your body meeting the earth's body.
Relax.
Feel those roots of yours.
Still reaching far down into the body of that place.
Sense how grounded
and held
and present you are.

Give thanks for this place,
in the way you know how.
For the more you can sense her aliveness,
the more you can sense your own.

Let yourself slowly rise to your feet
and walk from that place,
still aware that you're walking.
on her.

The Art of Arriving

So, please arrive.

Let yourself just sit for a while wherever you are.

As you can imagine, the act of arriving to a place is a genuinely underperformed art form. There's a style to it, a way to arrive that lets your body ease into the place you're arriving to. There's a grace and elegance to it, a feline sensibility, that invites you to relax into this transition—the coming out of somewhere and the coming into somewhere. In our case, the coming out of the wandering and the coming into a particular place.

There's no forcing or pushing or hurrying up to get there. Let it take all the time it needs. Contrary to the American industrial way, it is not efficient in the slightest. It is slow, like a well-cooked stew that finds its flavor over time. Arriving asks you to cease your journeying, put down your baggage or your basket, and be welcomed in. It says, relax and stay awhile.

So, wherever you are, be it on the sandy beach, grassy lawn, or forest floor, this practice asks you to learn the ways of arriving to that particular place. There's an almost forgotten clue embedded in the very word that remembers how to do so. The etymology and origin of the word *arrive* comes from Latin "ad ripam," which means "to the shore." The root of this word carries an old nautical memory of the end of a sailor's journey at sea, their heartbroken urge to come back to land, and the physical reunion of their body touching the shore's body again. Ugh, how gorgeous. The word is saturated with a profound sense of longing for the land they left and for the sweet relief of physically touching it again.

Whenever I settle down and practice this skill of arriving, I always sigh. Not intentionally, but as a consequence of planting myself on the earth and letting my body touch the ground again. The exhale softens my frazzled nerves and plugs me back into a greater, older life force. In today's manic, tech-driven age in which high speed is king and multitasking is queen, it's a profoundly somatic relief to have nowhere to be but exactly where I am. Sitting and sighing is my body's way of saying, "I'm here." It is the sound of my whole being coming ashore and letting the land hold me again.

Here versus There

I've been gathering teenagers around a fire for over ten years now.

Every Tuesday night we come together to light a fire and to listen to each other. We hold up enormous questions such as "What is love?" or "Am I in control of my life?" and stare into the fire, looking for insight in the flames. A few years ago, there was a boy named Ethan who came to the Fire Circle. Before anything was lit, he announced his attention deficit disorder in the same way someone in AA might introduce their addiction. "Hi, my name is Ethan and I can't pay attention." He was so earnest and self-aware. Yet he was also forewarning us that even though he was here with us, he was unreliable.

Now, attention deficit is not unusual for teenagers these days, or frankly for anyone who is plugged in to the modern media circus, like the attention draining, Facebooklandia. We have become a culture of distraction, unable or unwilling to be here because there's always the next thing to consume. Always hungry for the new and

the next, we have become a people who do not know how to be here.

As is tradition in the Fire Circle, we sparked the tinder first in silence. As it crackled into a warm blaze, Ethan's statement gave us something to wonder about: "Why are we so distracted nowadays?" and "What does it take to be here?" We put on more wood for such big questions. Going around the circle, the teens offered their troubled voices to what fueled the distractions in their lives. They spoke to their nagging fear of missing out (it's FOMO, Day <eye roll>), the unsettling belief that whatever they are or wherever they are "is not good enough," and the pressure they carry by attempting to do so many things at once. They spoke about their parents, counselors, and coaches who keep pushing them on to the next thing. But the trouble was that they didn't know where they were headed. The consequences, they said, was that so much of the time they don't fully feel present in anything they actually do.

This ciphering took hours until what was once hot and bright was just a twinkling of bright orange coals mirroring the stars overhead. It got quiet as it often does near the end, and Ethan, mesmerized by the movement of the dying fire, raised his hand without looking up and whispered, "Day, I think this is the first time I've paid attention for this long." My heart smiled. He was still here with us, dropped in and listening until the last coal went out. He had arrived.

And maybe you can try practicing this. Let yourself be here by giving up the notion of trying to be anywhere else for a while. Let *this* place be *the* place, at least for now. Wherever you are, it is enough. Don't let the seduction of a make-believe "there" be what pulls you out of the magic and intimacy of here. The place you are is longing for you to hear her voice, to bring her close, to let her touch you, change you. And, for her, you have the gift of your attention and senses.

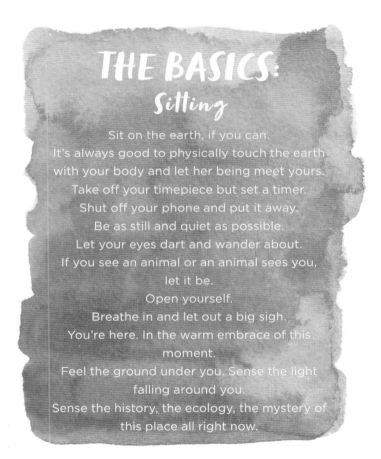

THE BASICS:
Sitting

Sit on the earth, if you can.
It's always good to physically touch the earth with your body and let her being meet yours.
Take off your timepiece but set a timer.
Shut off your phone and put it away.
Be as still and quiet as possible.
Let your eyes dart and wander about.
If you see an animal or an animal sees you, let it be.
Open yourself.
Breathe in and let out a big sigh.
You're here. In the warm embrace of this moment.
Feel the ground under you. Sense the light falling around you.
Sense the history, the ecology, the mystery of this place all right now.

chapter 3

CLEAR

**At the time of greatest vulnerability,
comes the clearest truth.**

—Joanna Macy

Revelation

Perhaps by now you've arrived in a particular spot. The more you sit with the place, the more is revealed. The more you observe of the place, the more you maybe see of yourself. There is the possibility of an endless reflection.

But now it's time for a revelation of your own. This is a kind of reveal that actually needs the use of your own hands. For at your very feet lies a hidden canvas—a blank slate buried beneath the branches and bark and bramble. The only thing you have to do is sweep away what covers and conceals it. You must reveal the "empty altar."

Chapter 3 is devoted to sweeping and preparing a bare earth altar. It may sound simple, but I warn you not to underestimate the power of this practice. Like a writer and her blank page or a choreographer and his empty dance studio, there's something enormously profound and terrifying about standing at the edge between nothing and everything. The unknown potential that exists before you begin to create can be paralyzing. There is so much to contend with. So much comes forward to clutter that space. So many fears and doubts appear. Impulses of procrastination and resistance can arrive. Thoughts of "I can't" or "It won't" can come to overwhelm the open canvas you just unveiled and block the creative impulses. With so much "me" in the way, how do you hear what is speaking to you under all of that?

This chapter puts a broom in your hand and helps to spark some courage in your heart. While we can't get rid of all fears and doubts, we can practice removing them from the center of your attention. This is not a guaranteed thing. I've made thousands of altars, and more often than not I am hit with a barrage of doubt as soon as I am faced with the empty space. It usually sounds like, "I don't know if I can do this again!" But the thing is, I brush aside the doubt and ask, plead, beg, and borrow to move myself out of the way. I seek a little more earth and a little less Day. I hope for a glimpse of insight. I tune my ear so that something or someone can speak to me through the empty space. On my best days, I can hear a whisper of it. Sweeping reveals the whisper.

I sweep to empty and I sweep to reveal. As Rumi says, emptiness "contains what you need." But is emptiness really empty? Could it be that emptiness is a channel through which your creative ideas can be conducted and transformed into action? Could it be that your creative ideas come from somewhere else and move through you to come into the world, meaning that your essential function is simply to keep the channel clear? We will soon find out.

So sweep, my friends. Reveal that bare earth canvas and practice moving yourself out of the way. We have too much "me" centeredness in our culture. Let's sweep the center and bring forth some bare and mysterious earth so that this art has a chance to come into this world for even the shortest amount of time. You stand boldly at the edge of nothing and everything. Sweep and stay open to it. Stay open. Stay open.

Clearing

Ready to clear some space for your altar?

Before you do, I want to make the case for you *not* to.

Or at least to consider something before you do.

You see, clearing can be a rather disruptive act, especially abrupt clearing. My ex-boyfriend is French. He would get unbelievably frustrated in American restaurants when the waitstaff came to clear the table the moment he put his fork down and finished eating. He felt insulted by this gesture and felt as if they wanted to rush him out so as to make room for the next customer. "It is so American," he would say in his incredibly adorable French accent, referencing the industrialized American culture that was always trying to make room for the new thing. From his perspective, the American way is to clear the table so that it can be made ready for the next customer.

My ex would tell me stories of dinners in Parisian restaurants that would last for hours. For better and worse, the servers would just forget about your table and leave your dishes exactly where they were until you got up from your seat and left the restaurant. Having an uncleared dirty dish was evidence that the meal was still happening.

This insight made me consider that perhaps what is to

be cleared shouldn't be cleared so haphazardly. There is such a thing here known as timing.

This is true for physical things as well as emotional and spiritual things. When you think you should "clean and cleanse" an area, I would ask you to take into consideration the very thing that you're longing to get rid of and to consider how much it has given you, despite your approval of it or not. For instance, whenever I find myself absolutely humbled by doubt, my first and persistent preference is, of course, to get rid of it. If I had a doubt vacuum, I would vacuum the bugger up in an instant so that I could proceed without it.

Doubt slows down everything and just doesn't feel good. The problem here is that when doubt arrives, especially when I'm creating my art, there are other qualities that can emerge as a consequence of it. Sometimes it looks like courage, and sometimes it feels like persistence, and other times it is like faith. Regardless, it is the doubt that brings forth these other attributes that I have come to see as gifts and skills.

If I cleared doubt the moment it arose, I wouldn't learn how to be courageous or persistent or faithful. And so I practice letting doubt linger just a little bit longer each and every time.

Listen, I am not suggesting to never clear anything immediately. Of course, there's a time and place for a quick clearing. For example, on a recent flight I embarrassingly spilt coffee all over my shirt. I was not going to let it soak me as I sat there wondering about the spiritual attributes of coffee—nor would you. You, like me, are going to clean it up as soon as possible.

Unlike cleaning up an accidental spill, however, there are times when we should not rush to clear away a space too soon. There are instances when you should let that

which you're eventually going to clear linger just a little longer. Why? Because the clutter is evidence that something happened, is maybe still happening, and perhaps still has something to say.

But so many of us are ruled by the mantra, "out with the old and in with the new." We consistently have our attention turned toward the novel and new, and we have a compulsive need to replace the old. We can witness this with the mad rush to buy a new phone, get a new car, or travel someplace new. We see this in Hollywood's obsession with new talent and the fashion industry's focus on the latest and hottest trends.

It's especially devastating to observe how our culture treats our elders and seniors who are often pushed aside and made irrelevant, even as they are seduced into trying to look and act young.

Yet in traditional and indigenous cultures, it is the other way around entirely. Elders come first. Their gray hair and wrinkles are evidence that life has happened. Those people who have sustained themselves over time carry enormous value for the culture, and the youth are taught to offer gifts, patience, and respect for their beloved elderly ones.

To have an elder in your midst is considered to be a blessing. They have lived through the beginning and middle of their lives, and they are evidence of the beauty and wisdom that is found in an ending.

Endings are all around us. And in our practice, they are right under your feet. They tell the story of what once was and what will become. Practice having your attention turned toward those endings. Wonder about them. Listen to the story they are singing to you as they change. And don't supplant what is there yet with your newest expression. Learn about what you are about to clear. Let them linger a little longer.

I love watching the altars I make decompose over time. I often return to the same spot, and before me are the shriveled flowers, the crunched pinecones, and the chomped acorns that I meticulously placed the day before. But what I had so carefully arranged is now a big mess. Of course, my first instinct is to swipe it all away, because it's a new day and it's time for a new altar. Plus, it's decaying and has lost the exactitude that I originally intended. But this instinct is careless. It's the same impulse that makes us want to clear away those dirty dishes immediately—the same sentiment that encourages us to believe that the old has no place or purpose. This is the trance of our modern world, and it seduces us into a certain kind of amnesia in which we worship the next and newest, while we forget to value what came before.

The dried leaves, the broken branches, the devoured berries, and the wilted flowers, all of this mess is evidence of a life and a journey. They were all once fresh, green leaves, whole and vibrant branches, and stunning flowers. And they still carry the remnants of that earlier life. They are evidence of what is to eventually become of the material for my new altar. All of the fresh flowers that I foraged for today's altar will soon enough look like the wilted flowers from yesterday's altar. It's the beautiful cycle right before me. The old is the reminder to you that says, slow down and linger for as long as possible.

There is a Japanese tradition called kintsugi where instead of throwing away broken pottery, it is glued back together. Its practitioners then line the cracked edges in dusted gold to accentuate the places where the pottery had broken. I'm told that this gold honors and remembers the journey of that particular pot or bowl. The craftwork is evidence that the piece had been well loved and now carries a story. This tradition is an antidote for the modern person's addiction to always longing for the new when the old is broken or outdated. It suggests that the older we get, the more beautiful we can become. It says, don't throw me away just yet.

With my Morning Altars, I have a ritual of sitting, brush in hand, pausing and taking in the place as it is before I sweep it away. I intentionally hold this clearing instrument but don't immediately rush into the act of clearing. This is my way of honoring all that has come before. To pause with my brush lets me linger a little bit longer with the way it is. All of it. It lets there be space before the next new thing arrives. It is the space between something ending and something beginning. There's such beauty and sorrow and wisdom in that.

Only then do I sweep. As I'm writing this, I'm aware of how close the word *sweep* and *weep* are. I am reminded of the beautiful heartbreak that comes with having to clear away something so beautiful, something that you wish could exist forever, like that night at a Parisian restaurant. It's a beautiful thing to clear in this way—with a long slow approach—to welcome in the new altar in the presence and love of what has come before.

When I Learned to Sweep Beautifully

I always have a small hand broom in my basket. When I first began my Morning Altars practice, it was a cheap plastic one that you can get at a dollar store. I used it so much, and in places that it was never meant to be used, that it eventually snapped in two. Since then, I've procured an antique hand broom. Its silver handle is etched

with a woman praising the sky and its base is made of neatly wrapped grass bristles all woven precisely together. This hand broom is from another time when things were made well and makers took great pride in their craftwork.

I found it displayed on a table with women's vanity items from the 1920s at the local antique fair that happens on the first Sunday of every month. I was moved to buy it. It was elegant, sturdy, and would seriously up my game when sweeping. I wondered: Would having a beautiful broom have an impact on my art? If my tools were beautiful, I asked myself, would that benefit the beauty I made? I decided to upgrade the hand broom and find out.

The next morning, I walked down the path toward the creek near my home to build a new altar. I sat near the creek, that was almost silent due to that season's drought. I noticed that the forest floor was blanketed with fresh dead leaves. This is not unusual, especially for that time of the year when the bay laurel and redwood trees shed their growth, covering all of the dry earth. And, as I like to do, I sat with the place for some time, looking around to see if the two silly squirrels that love to chase each other in spirals up and down the redwood tree were there. No such luck. As I relaxed and arrived, I remembered how blessed I was to be able to call this place home. I like to begin creating when I'm filled with some gratitude for life.

I took out my new old-time, silver-handled, sky woman hand broom and remembered the question that came to me the day before: How would having a beautiful broom impact my art? I paused before I swept and took in all that had come before. Yet, it seemed like there was now something about holding her that made my approach to

the earth and my art carry a little more heft and elegance in a way the dollar store brush could never accomplish.

I began to clear and sweep the earth, and I heard her bristles make that beautiful whispering song that was being sung as a duet with the ground: "shhee, shhee—shhee, shhee." I cleared all the leaves and berries and bark until there was just bare earth. Because I was finally sweeping with a fancier broom, and not a flimsy one, it seemed that the sweeping wasn't just a practical matter anymore. It had become a ritualized way of preparing for the art. The hand broom upgrade was tutoring me in a preparation upgrade. I was learning that my entire approach mattered, that my whole way could be filled with beauty. Of course the broom was just an instrument, but it was honing my attention to the ways of sweeping: the pause I take before sweeping, how I hold the broom, the way I kneel down on the earth, the song I sing or thoughts I think while I sweep, the direction I sweep in. All of this was fair game, an invitation to approach with more courtesy and consciousness, and a reminder that this sweeping ritual was really a way of courting beauty and the Earth. Beauty making does not begin when you create your first mark. It begins by your approach toward the beauty itself—and toward the Earth herself.

All of this came through that little broom. Such quiet, elegant wisdom passed through my hands from the silver-handled hand broom etched with the woman praising the sky. And, perhaps, this woman was practicing her own kind of beautiful approach as well.

Grasping

So here's a practice for you: When you clear the ground, practice how you hold the broom. If you don't have a broom, don't worry—you can do this with your hands. My good friend and author Matthew Stillman taught me this practice when referencing how tightly people grasp their pen while writing. He said that the way you hold your pen effects not only what you write but also your experience of writing. He suggested the same was true for a broom.

Let's begin.

Start off by gripping the broom as hard as you can. Grind the broom into the earth and apply maximum pressure with all your force. What is the experience like? How much are you able to sweep? What does this do to the broom? How much impact are you making on the earth? If you're using your hand, brush the earth with the same intensity.

Now reduce the pressure by 10 percent. Same thing. Sweep with a little less force but still forcing it. Ask yourself the same questions.

Reduce the pressure by 10 percent increments, until you're gripping the broom with only 10 percent of your force. You will be barely holding the broom. Again, what is this experience like? How much are you able to sweep and what kind of impact are you making? If you're using your hand, what does it feel like to brush the earth ever so slightly?

Once you've gone down to that 10 percent threshold, go back and find the appropriate amount of tension for you. How much do you need to bring for the sweeping to be done well? Remember the point here is not for you to do a good job of sweeping, but rather for you to find

a way for the sweeping to be an extension of your mind and behavior.

Consider this exercise as a way to strengthen your sensitivity muscle that allows beauty to come in all by itself. Let the act of sweeping be a beauty-making endeavor of its own.

Too often we think we need to exert maximum effort, because we think that only through force and strain will beauty appear. Sometimes we even think we can bring it in all by ourselves.

Please consider this as a way to prepare your hands and mind for greater sensitivity and the upcoming act of creating and arranging. I have squished so many berries when trying to place them on an altar because my mind was overpowering the sensitivity of my hands and the delicateness of the material.

How hard we try is not always the most effective way. Sometimes, we need to learn how to meet something with as little of ourselves as we can so that the beauty can arrive on its own.

Let the Dust Settle

After you clear the earth, let the dust settle.

I'll explain.

I worked for a decade in the theater, and during those years a new and unfortunate phenomenon began, with regard to standing ovations. Apparently, every show now deserved them. But it's not just the ovation that changed but the timing. The lights go down and, almost instantly, there's applause. It's as if the audience must immediately fill the theater with the sound of their approval, leaving no doubt that they loved it. All this applause is definitely courteous, but it also has a generic quality to it. I have no problem with immediate applause if it's genuine. But there is another way. And it's incredibly powerful. Holy even.

A few years back, I attended a four-and-a-half-hour production of Eugene O'Neill's *Long Day's Journey into Night* on Broadway. In the last moment of the play Vanessa Redgrave descends a staircase, lost in her character's drugged trance. As the lights came down, not a sound was heard in the house. Over a thousand people, sat in stunned silence. The ending of this great masterpiece just reverberated like a gong. No one applauded. Everyone sat at the edge of their seats letting the silence speak and build into a palpable tension that could not be contained. Then the applause rushed through the house, which was like letting loose a cannon of pressure that had been building up during four and a half hours, as we erupted into a shouting kind of praise. I've never been a part of anything like that before, a moment as riveting as the entire performance. The silence before the applause was so alive, whole, and beautiful.

During some classical music concerts, this is actually the etiquette. At the end of any performance, silence precedes applause. There are some conductors who won't lower their arms until there is enough time to let the music settle. In a way, they go from conducting the orchestra to conducting the audience so as to allow the fullness of the ending to happen. That silence gives room for the ending before the audience fills that space with their voice. There is deep listening being practiced in that silence. And a skill to be able to hear the departure of the music and some discretion to not let your voice rush to dominate that space.

So when I say let the dust settle after you sweep your circle of bare earth, it is an invitation for you to practice being utterly still and attentive to the swept space. Don't just clear it and then immediately start arranging your altar. Put down your broom, or if you cleared with your hands, put them down too, and just let it be. Observe what you just did. Look at your brushstroke on the earth. See the shape of the circle you made. Listen to the sounds that occur after you swept. Observe how your movement of clearing is in itself a whole and complete expression. In a way, a cleared space is an entire altar. Perhaps you do not need to add anything to it. Perhaps it is your very first altar. What does it say to you?

One time, I hiked into a redwood forest in Mendocino, California, and simply cleared a circle on the forest floor without building an altar on top of it. I spent hours slowly preparing the space. I let the movement of the clearing be my meditation and the empty space itself be my offering and altar. I withheld my desire to fill the circle with anything and just let the space I cleared be enough. Afterward, I walked atop a nearby hill, looked down, and witnessed something so remarkably simple and beautiful: emptiness within fullness. A carefully cleared circle silently singing within a forest densely carpeted in leaves.

In many ways, this practice is similar to the Japanese calligraphic ensō circles, or zen circles, which are made by monks or nuns who, after meditating sometimes over months with extreme discipline, hold a paintbrush drenched in ink and, with one solid stroke, paint a circle that represents his or her profound essence. The stroke is a symbol of wholeness and completion, and the cyclical nature of existence. None are the same and each one is quite striking. The circles themselves are not designed to be perfect but rather are perfect reflections of the painter's state of mind. They are exercises in transmitting the quality of attentiveness and inner stillness of the monk or nun.

When we clear a circle on the earth, we are expressing our inner state. It is the evidence of how we are bringing ourselves to the earth. To let the dust settle afterward is to allow this clearing to be complete in and of itself. This exercise contends with an immediate desire to make it more than it is—"But it's just a cleared circle"—and to get to the real altar that is filled with the beautiful things you foraged.

But remember, this is a real altar. In our Western culture, we struggle with this—we're always rushing to fill something, do something, make something, fix something, say something. As a result we are almost unaware of the space prior to the doing, making, fixing, or saying as being anything that is relevant or worthy. It's almost as if we can only see ourselves if we see what we've done to the thing rather than being in the presence of what we have yet to do.

For instance, my best friend recently got into a fight with his partner. He found it incredibly challenging to let there be some quiet space afterward. He wanted to rush in immediately and attempt to fix or remedy the situation because he was uncomfortable with the space. But if he allowed the dust to settle, he would be able to see that within that space is a whole realm of reflection that can inform him of the ways he approached the relationship in the first place.

> A circle as a vast space,
> which does not lack anything,
> nor does it have too much.
>
> —*Shin Jin Mei*

Another example. You send a text message to a new love interest. There is no response for a few hours. Now be honest: How hard is it for you to allow some space between responses? How often are you checking your phone to see if they wrote back? How tempted are you to write them again asking if they received your message?

As an artist and writer, I am often con-fronted by this before I create anything. My mind has a habit of being pretty intolerant toward the empty canvas or page, and so it rushes in to fill it with anything. The consequences are that my mind is always center stage, which doesn't allow for anything else to be there. And if that space is occupied, then there is no room for any unknown creative urges to come in from beyond.

So let it settle. Let the earth be unfilled for some time. Let the space you cleared be an expression of your mind and heart. Our approach impacts every step of our altar-making journey. Put the broom (or your hands) down and be in the presence of your ensō circle. Be present to your inner state, which is made manifest into a mark on the earth's ground.

A Wild Strawberry Center

One summer I taught in Squaw Valley, California, at the Wanderlust Festival, which is a gathering dedicated to yoga, music, and evolving consciousness. Squaw Valley is the site where the 1960 Winter Olympic Games were held, and it is an absolutely stunning place with steep valleys that rise and fall at the foot of a towering rocky mountain. To get to the top, you and 30 other people pack into an enormous roomlike tram that is like riding in an old-school version of Roald Dahl's *Charlie and the Great Glass Elevator*. The ride is nerve-racking, because you wonder with reasonable trepidation how this woven chord of wire can carry so much weight; but it is also enjoyable, because you get to see the mountain in ways you never could from the base: pine trees proudly growing out of rock cliffs and little patches of scattered and densely packed ice that look like solar panels embedded on the mountain. As we arrived at the top, I met up with my group for our day-long forage and altar-building workshop. A not too shabby view for the day's proceedings.

Karen, one of the workshop participants, was someone who stood out. She was a fast-talking, highly caffeinated, and rather hilarious lawyer from New York City. For someone moving so fast, I could tell this altar-making practice was going to be good for her, provided that she allowed herself to slow down and be with the process and the mountain. As we gathered around for introductions, she let it be known to both me and the group that she was unsure if this was the right workshop for her as she claimed to not have a creative bone in her body. She didn't know exactly why she was there but was willing to at least try it out. When people tell me they aren't creative and, therefore, can't build an altar, I often push back. From my perspective, altar building is probably the best medicine for people who don't consider themselves creative because it's impossible to mess up. Half of the beauty making already has been achieved thanks to the abundant generosity of the earth. The creative act is simply in the arrangement of that beauty. So with a little nudging from me and her own willingness to understand why the fates brought her there, Karen and the group went off to forage and build their altars to adorn the mountainside.

A couple of hours later, the group gathered. But there was no sign of Karen.

We reluctantly proceeded without her company only to find her 20 minutes later nestled between two large boulders that formed a little A-frame. She was hunched over, still meticulously creating her altar. Watching Karen was like watching a child completely immersed building a sandcastle. Her focus was absolutely honed, and she was so engrossed in the creative act that she didn't even hear us approach or sit down. When she finally looked up, Karen saw us and we saw her. She looked like a person who just had a revelation. With tears welling up in her eyes, she revealed to us that, even though she's resisted it for many years now, she is understanding herself to be a hoarder. Her home is cluttered with too many things and she has a lot of trouble throwing anything away, because holding on to things makes her feel safe and comfortable. But it also leaves a lot of consequences in her life, particularly her inability to find partnership.

Earlier in the day, when I introduced the group to the third movement of building a Morning Altar, the act of clearing a circle, Karen said she didn't take much notice of it. But when she sat down under those two boulders that formed a little roof over her head, she couldn't stop

clearing. She cleared and cleared and got into the meditation of it, slowing down to move each rock, one by one, which she said felt like it was clearing her mind as well. Apparently, she got so taken by the clearing exercise that she surrendered to it. She thought that the act of clearing would be her entire altar-making experience. And she was glad with that. It brought her peace and inspired her to approach her home and her habits again with renewed effort when she went back to New York. But, unexpectedly, toward the last bit of clearing, Karen caught a little dash of red that was playing a peak-a-boo with her. Her curiosity was piqued, and she slowly unearthed what was blocking it and revealed a patch of ripe and unripe, wild strawberries that were hidden at the base of the

rock. Karen explained, through her tears, that she wasn't expecting there to be such a surprise of beauty revealed to her through her efforts of clearing. The beauty was there all along, she just couldn't see it.

Underneath those two boulders, Karen devoted her handiwork to a commitment to make room for the beauty that was trying to come into her life and into the world. We all gathered around Karen and put our hands on her in silence and let her spoken prayer be witnessed by all of us. We then put our hands on the earth to consider that the moment may have even been witnessed by the very mountain herself. We were all touched that a little hidden patch of wild strawberries could make such a profound impact.

Being a Conductor

That experience with Karen left a mark on my life. I don't believe that ideas originate within me but rather, if I do the deep work of creating space by getting out of the way and quieting my mind, sometimes, on those rare and remarkable days, they arrive and pay me a visit.

As an artist, I like to think of myself as a conductor, a person who is open to receiving new inspirations and visions. There's an interesting correlation between the words *conduct* and *conduit*. Both mean to lead or to guide, and that serves as a clue for understanding the purpose of our behavior. Our conduct, the way we express ourselves through our approach, our attentiveness, and our willingness, impacts what we can receive. Our behavior and approach can very much open us up as a channel. A conductive approach doesn't guarantee that we will receive anything grand or epic, and that's not the point. Rather, we must be willing to refine the way we carry ourselves, because there's an understanding that we are a conduit for a greater expression, a channel for, what author Elizabeth Gilbert calls "big magic" that can move through us and into the world.'

Martha Graham, the choreographer of modern dance, spoke about this channel to Agnes deMille: "There is

a vitality, a life force, an energy, a quickening that is translated through you into action, and because there is only one of you in all of time, this expression is unique. And if you block it, it will never exist through any other medium and it will be lost. The world will not have it. It is not your business to determine how good it is nor how valuable nor how it compares with other expressions. It is your business to keep it yours clearly and directly, to keep the channel open. You do not even have to believe in yourself or your work. You have to keep yourself open and aware to the urges that motivate you. Keep the channel open.... No artist is pleased. [There is] no satisfaction whatever at any time. There is only a queer divine dissatisfaction, a blessed unrest..."

I adore this wisdom because it reminds me how essential it is to maintain an opening through which the mystery and the Earth can speak to me. "Keep the channel open" reminds me that an artist must practice, which is one of maintenance—an action of clearing a space, both internally and externally, so that those creative urges may enter. This is why I sweep before I create my altar. I sweep so as to let there be room for a greater inspiration to enter.

And I sweep so that I may remember I am a conduit for it.

THE BASICS:
Clearing

Come with a small hand broom, branch,
or just use your hands!

Don't clear yet. Pause before you sweep and
presence all that came before you.

Sweeping isn't just functional;
it's an act of beauty.

As you sweep, observe how you sit,
how you hold the broom or your hand, what
thoughts come into your head. Let the whole
experience be mindful.

Create a circle of bare earth—your canvas.

Pause after you sweep.
Be in the presence of what is yet to come.

Let there be space.

chapter 4

CREATE

The aim of art is to represent not the outward appearance of things, but their inward significance.

—Aristotle

Just Begin

This is the creative moment. Now your imagination gets to play with the Earth's creations.

You've wandered and foraged, arrived and listened. You've cleared the space and now your hands get to adorn her in beauty. There's no right way to do it. So please free yourself from any expectation that it needs to look a certain way. There's no way to know anything here in advance. This is purely a process of discovery.

Too often we come to a moment of creativity and hesitate because our minds speak louder than our hearts. There's the figure-it-out mind that wants to know everything before doing it. There's the judgmental mind that compares itself to others. There's the disbelieving mind that stops us before we begin, because "I could never." And there's the fearful "what if" mind that warns us of the perils of making a mistake. Our minds can become such enormous roadblocks that prevent us from expressing ourselves freely. When blocked, we never get to encounter the effortless grace that is capable of flowing through our expression, an expression that is so desperately needed in this world.

In the face of all of the many reasons not to, of all the ways we can overthink, doubt, dismiss, and hesitate, the directive here is to just begin. Put something down. The beauty contained in a single leaf can evaporate all of the mind's chatter. It is the simple things we need more of these days. Simple action, simple movement, simple choices. This is where we can locate our humanity again, which is too often lost in an overly complex world. Put something down and let it speak to you. So much of what we're trying so hard to figure out is often right before us. There is nothing here that needs to be considered too deeply. Just begin tangibly and begin simply. The simplest of beginnings have a compelling voice of their own.

You'll find that one thing leads to the next. You put something down and then another. This is a one-step-at-a-time process that unfolds as you engage it. And as it moves, you must stay with it. You're not meant to know where you're going in advance, so forget that. Just keep exploring and let every step of this practice inform the next step. It is an experiment of trying and seeing—of placing something down and maybe picking something up. There isn't anything more than that. It's filled with mistakes that aren't even mistakes, because each step informs what comes next. It's a journey that you can happily get lost in.

And that's the point. Keep going until you are taken with the beauty that is unfolding before you. As you continue to move, let your heart be your guide. Let your eyes widen. Let your hands arrange. Quiet that mind of yours so that something can take shape before you that you never even intended. That's the mysterious beauty of this creative practice. That is the treasure redeemed—as it takes on a life of its own and as you become its midwife, carefully bringing it into this world with your attentiveness and grace. Soon enough, what exists before you, made at your very feet and with your very hands, is a reflection of your imaginative spirit coming alive through the imagination of the Earth. Maybe this is what it looks like to let the Earth dream through your hands.

can we speak in flowers.
it will be easier for me
to understand.

—*Nayyirah Waheed*

It's All Play

Okay, before I go on, I should probably issue a fair warning: This chapter will not contain a "Here's how you build an altar" formula that I concocted from all my tireless research of sacred geometry and mathematical equations, which I tested thoroughly, and that, if you do it the way I tell you to, will guarantee a beautiful and sacred altar. That is not going to happen in this book. Actually, most of the time I only realize what I did after it happened. The recipe creates itself in the moment. Put another way, there is no predetermined way to build a Morning Altar, but there is an infinite number of ways to arrange beauty. So the focus of this chapter is not going to be on how to produce a beautiful product, but instead it will ask you to learn how to let the process unfold beautifully. You really can't mess this up, but if you're only looking for the right way to do this, then that might just be the way to do so.

Here's what I will tell you: The most useful skill to employ when creating altars is play. Like a kid in a sandbox, the play lets me get lost in the world that I am playing within. It becomes an experience that I can be immersed in for hours. My hands are arranging, my mind is attentive, and time stands still. Again, as with the other Morning Altar processes, I'm not trying to get somewhere. Play is all journey. Any destination I come to is purely temporary. Why? Because the play happens when I'm exploring and experimenting. The play wants to keep the game alive, and for as long as possible. So let me be clear: I do not create so I can have a finished altar. I create so I can explore the world I am creating within. Anything that is made is simply a consequence of my commitment to stay in the play.

And what keeps the play playing are the endless possibilities to explore. No altar is too big and no altar is too small. I make rules and break them all the time. The play keeps tempting me to find novel ways of expressing an idea or a pattern. I often sense that I am being tutored by the Earth herself, who is always pushing the limits of what is possible. She directly confronts my rational mind that is already trying to say "I can't" or "It won't." That mindset always chooses defeat in the face of challenge, because it thinks that just because it hasn't happened yet means that it will never happen. The Earth is always teaching me otherwise: to always push, try, peal, invent, and keep stretching the boundaries of beauty.

There was the springtime, for instance, when I foraged a huge stem of Echium candicans, otherwise known as pride of Madeira, that had been plant roadkill. These guys are tall, towering stalks with little flowers that spiral up their shaft. And it was the color of the flowers that drew my eye. But the size, almost 3 feet tall, was way too big for the altar. No matter how many times I tried to arrange that enormous plant, it didn't work. It didn't seem to play nicely with its altar-neighbors and just dominated the space. So instead of giving up on it, I chose to play with it, turn it, open it, deconstruct it, and see what came to life that way. Well, wouldn't you know that this enormous stalk consisted of clusters of the most interesting, pinky-size green fiddleheads, each with a little sprout of periwinkle tuft on its head, like a mini-mohawk. I pulled each of these fiddleheads apart from the stem. Their individual shapes were so interesting. They sang to me. And not just a sweet little tune but an entire opera. They just had this old world romantic feel to them. When I laid them head to head, they appeared as these little green heart shapes; and when I laid them tail to tail, they made a very fancy

calligraphic *S*—shapes that I never would have thought possible from this big obtuse plant. And, as I arranged these little fiddleheads, a broader pattern opened up in my imagination, which took me back in time to the intricate art nouveau style of the late 1800s. An unexpected world was coming alive to me, all because of a desire to push the limits of a flower.

As you can tell, it's important for me to have material that I love playing with. This is the magic of collaborating with the Earth as opposed to working with paints or pencils. The Earth is playing too by creating such amazing shapes, textures, colors, and designs, some that are quite hidden. The game becomes one of trying to discover them or, even better, trying to make them look like something else. Creativity is not only about generating something new from scratch. It is also about playing with the pieces that are already here and discovering new ways for them to express themselves. I think it's why so many kids love to play with Legos. They get to work with blocks, and through the wondrous ways they arrange, build, and stack them, they can produce something unexpected.

Pushing the limits of what is possible is one of my favorite games of artistic play. Try this with a leaf. Cut it, fold it, or arrange it differently so that it looks like something else entirely. I've taken rib bones and made them look like a boat's propellers; I've used the helicopter seed pods of a maple tree and arranged them like lattice work. Play and imagination are what make these transformations possible. Anything can become anything else, and the invisible can be made visible.

Once I found a half-eaten pinecone that a squirrel must have chewed on, as each of the pinecone's petals were laying all around it. While it is incredibly difficult to pull pinecone petals apart with your own bare hands, the squirrel did me the favor. I noticed that each petal had a little white teardrop groove embedded in it, which is where the seed must have slept. While I've created many altars with pinecones, I had never created one just with their petals. I was so inspired. I arranged them on the ground, putting the petals in a circle shape, and without even realizing it, each of those white teardrop grooves created its own circle within the circle. The shapes were playing and evolving with each other, some intended and others by complete surprise. That is the magic of discovering the unpredictable beauty in nature, which is so healthy for us humans.

Playing is an act of animating that surprise. It beckons everything to come alive and play back with you. Or rather, it asks you to leave behind your own convincing disbelief and remember how alive everything is already. This is the dichotomy presented in Antoine de Saint-Exupéry's classic *The Little Prince,* where he suggests that as we age we have trouble holding on to our sense of wonderment and possibility. We adults cultivate mindsets that limit our childlike imagination for the sake of achievement, success, and control. As a result we become blasé to the living, changing world around us. To redeem our innate sense of curiosity, we must question the mindset that traps us in a very lonely and predictable world. Question the blasé! And we do this by wondering about everything around us. When I can question my own limiting adult perspective, I can begin to see beyond it and to connect back again with the animate world. No longer am I only hearing my own voice but instead I

co-exist in a world where everything speaks with its own unique, quirky, gorgeous personality. Every berry has a little voice, every grass stalk makes itself known. I become surrounded by a community of living Earth, and this entire community is willing to play with me in this changing game of life.

Let's remember that this is a practice and that there's nothing here, especially play, that we need to do right. While making the art, I can't count how many times I've realized that I had stopped playing and had become incredibly serious and rigid. My hands were grasping too tightly. My eyes were clenched. My whole body was forcing the process. In those moments, I had lost the playful rhythm and had become consumed with the drumbeat of "should." In such moments, I get these preconceived notions of what should be happening or where things should be, which is a good indicator that my perfectionist self is trying to dominate the game. It means that I have fallen out of the journey and instead have become focused on the illusion of trying to get somewhere I should be.

So the practice is to reign in my perfectionist in these moments and to remind him that there's no "there." There's only here. And everything here is part of this process. Becoming good at playing takes practice, and some of the best ways to get skillful at playing is to recognize when you've stopped playing. In those moments, I usually laugh and remind myself that I'm making art with nature. It's not that serious, kiddo.

Play is a path toward release. And being creative still comes down to my willingness to let go and allow the experience to come to life. If I were to sit down and try to figure it all out beforehand, I would drive myself mad. Instead, I play as a way to loosen my tight grip on how I think things should be, and I let myself relax and witness what is born from that very place.

> No great artist ever sees things as they really are. If he did, he would cease to be an artist.
> —Oscar Wilde

Creating from the Center

As I said, there are no rules here. There are no prescriptions, must dos, or paint-by-number instructions that will present you with a beautiful but generic expression. I am attempting to describe and not prescribe the process so you can find your own way into it, so you can fall in love with it. Imagine me in the branches of that tree you sit underneath, like a little wood elf, rooting for you to take a chance and to express that gorgeous heart of yours with the land. I'm whispering to you: Just try!

Sometimes I meet someone, maybe even someone like you, who is absolutely unsure how to begin. Their uncertainty is so strong that it defeats them entirely. Perhaps it is the thought of starting that seems too overwhelming to them, or maybe they believe they couldn't create anything of substance, and so they give up before they even start. "Why even give it a go?" they ask. It's so easy to be a victim of our own fear of beginning something. That initial movement makes us feel so utterly

vulnerable because it threatens us with rejection. There have been more men than I can count that I have never asked on a date because I was too scared to make the first move.

And, by the way, count me in among those of you who are unsure of how to begin making an altar. I often have thoughts running through my mind suggesting that I quit before I begin. The most popular rerun sounds a little like this: "Yeah, you did it before but you can't do it again." Ouch. Rejected before I even get started. Oh, man, does that one freeze me in my tracks. How do I even respond to that?

But, wouldn't you know it, my response is actually a rather rebellious one. I move right up against the face of that debilitating block, and I respond with a simple and powerful act of resistance.

I begin. And I start in the center.

Rather than trying to placate my fears or overly psychologize them, I just put something down. Great rebellions have begun this way. I drop something in the center, like a pebble in a pond, and watch it ripple outward. Putting something tangibly down is a sign that a move has been made. Perhaps it leads only to the next step, but frankly that is how the entire thing will be built. Beginning in the center is not a steadfast rule and I don't always obey it; however, it is the secret weapon I employ against this block. It guides me through my fears and

brings me back to the earth. It quite literally grounds the process.

Tending to the center is a meditation. It becomes the central place that gives focus, both for the piece and for my own peace of mind. The thinking mind often flits and flirts in a million and one directions, and it needs an actual point to concentrate on in order to be still. When I establish a center, it becomes the focal point that I can attend to, observe, and create from. Everything then evolves from there. After I complete a large, quite intricately designed altar, it's remarkable to remember that it began from a simple centerpiece, a small circle of berries perhaps.

Once a year, I attend a 10-day silent meditation retreat called Vipassana. It's a profound and often challenging way to come to understand the movements and temperaments of my mind and ego. For 12 hours a day, we sit in meditation and learn how to train the mind to peacefully and attentively observe the sensations of the body. For the first six days, we are taught a technique called Anapana, which is simply to watch the breath come and go. The nose and nostril become our center point to observe as our body breathes, and we practice keeping our vigilant attention there. When it's distracted, we simply return to that place. Of course, the challenge is to train your attention to rest in one place, and it's often a constant tug of war between an agitated mind and a focused

one. There is no doubt that my mind will wander, forget, and get lost in thoughts of the past and future. But the key is to return to that center.

In the same way, your altar's center can be a place to return to. As you arrange outward, let the center do what it wants to do, which is to anchor and focus both the altar and your attention. Since the center is the origin of your arrangement, the place where it began, it's a good practice to continue to return your attention there. Let the center of your altar be a focal point of concentration. As you continue to arrange your altar, it is the center that all the patterns emerge from. By letting the center speak, you are allowing your creation to be well integrated and balanced. For example, I sometimes do this with color. If I place a brilliant purple thistle blossom in the center, I will let that color of the center speak throughout the entire piece like a common thread. I find the same is true for our lives. Tending to our places of origin—letting our attention return to the places that center us and give us life, be

it our breath, our Earth, our ancestors, our bodies—brings balance to our life as well.

A few summers ago I created a 20-foot circular Morning Altar in Mont-Tremblant, Canada. It eventually came to look like a spiraling wheel filled with crabapples, sunflower petals, flat cedar leaf, and many, many other materials. But this altar did not begin with any blueprint or masterplan. Instead, it started as a big stinking mess. When I began, I started in many directions at once. Maybe I was tired from all the traveling, or because I was feeling the pressure of having to build something large that would be seen by thousands of people. Whatever the reason, I put crab apples in one place and then switched my attention to a totally different spot where I did something random with sand. In retrospect, this was a pure reflection of my distracted mental state. And, because I'm rather bullheaded, I committed myself to this multidirectional, sporadic way for the entire first day. By sundown, the altar was truly all over the place and so were my nerves. I was freaking out. I only had one more day to complete this piece and I had no idea where I was going with it at all.

So the next day I awoke before dawn and got myself down to the land. I cleared away all of the hours of work I arranged the day before, and then I sat with the place in the dark and collected my thoughts. I sat with all the worries, fears, concerns, and doubts that arose and had been dragging me all over the place. And then I meditated. I focused my attention on my breath to center me. I let my nervous, anxious mind return to a calm state by concentrating on one constant thing, my breath. And I did this until the morning light grew. Eventually, I relaxed. I then let this clear mind help me begin again. I placed an Echinops bannaticus flower, otherwise known as a blue globe in the center. That dramatic and prickly flower was my anchor and origin. Everything came from there. While still concentrating on my breath, I let the spiraling wheel unfold from that one place. And after some time, the altar finally began to take shape and come alive. That day, I again understood the symbiotic relationship between my own centeredness and the altar's center. They truly are a reflection of each other.

The Ripples

From the center comes movement. Whatever that center is, be it a flower, a river stone, or the negative space that is created when the outline of two maple leaves come together, something happens on its own. I call it ripples. In a way, the center pulses outward and other shapes or patterns emerge from there. The center point, like in a lotus flower, inspires growth and expansion.

As on the smooth expanse of crystal lakes; the sinking stone at first a circle makes, the trembling surface by the motion stirr'd, spreads in a second circle, then a third; wide, and more wide, the floating rings advance, fill all the wat'ry plain, and to the margin dance.
—*Alexander Pope*

From that one place comes many ripples. I think about all the ancient myths, from Jewish to Hindu, that begin with a sound or word that ripples outward to create the entire universe. Your altar is a tiny little universe, and the center of it is where it all began.

From your center, new choices present themselves—choices that you may not even have considered beforehand. A flower center may lead to some grasses forming a diamond shape around the flower, which may lead to a trail of berries that ripple out from there, and so on. When we make a choice, other choices arise as a consequence. Intuition and creativity really ask us to listen and witness the way our choices expand outward and make impact.

The poet Alexander Pope delightfully speaks to what I'm talking about. When we drop a stone in a lake, it brings movement and consequence. That one drop doesn't just create one rippling ring but it keeps rippling, creating circle after circle that moves outward. In the tossing of that stone you create a trail of expanding circles on the water, which is evidence of your influence on the lake. But if you listen to your intuition, it will tell you that rather than

the rippling effect being random, those ripples expand equally. This insight reveals a secret of the universe—that life is moving in patterns. Those ripples on the water are one way nature makes invisible forces visible. We can see this play of rippling patterns all over nature in the form of craters, bubbles, flowers, and exploding stars. Our entire Milky Way galaxy is one expanding ripple!

Cymatics is a really fascinating way to understand this. In 1680, a man by the name of Robert Hooke took a violin bow and ran it along the edge of a glass plate covered with flour. He played the bow and observed nodal patterns emerge in the flour. Basically, he was able to see that sound itself forms mandala-like patterns on its own. The flour just revealed the patterns already there. You can try this at home: Take a handful of any small particle—sand, dust, or metal filings—and put it

on a metal plate with a speaker underneath. Depending on the different frequencies coming from the speaker, the sand or other substances are naturally organized into different geometrical shapes and patterns. In other words, the invisible sounds have visible shapes, which are intricate and gorgeous.

You are learning the language of the universe just by arranging your altar. It is spoken through symmetrical shapes and patterns. You get to bring your own unique expression to a universal one. I think this is why I adore symmetry so much in my art. When I look at it, my eyes can rest in the unfolding pattern and my soul can breathe because I'm speaking with the language of life. My deep affinity for symmetrical patterns isn't unique—you can find cultures all over the world that express geometrical and symmetrical patterns in their fabrics, beadwork, pottery, mosaics, and paintings. The Shipibo people of Peru make the most gorgeous, intricately sewed fabric of symmetrical patterns that are inspired by the visions they receive while drinking the traditional medicine brew, ayahuasca. Clearly, there's a collective understanding that these patterns are telling us a bigger story of the expanding universe we live in.

While I never would consider myself a math person, not even in the slightest, my art is pure mathematics. The word *mathema* signifies "learning in general," and it is the root of the Old English *mathein*, meaning "to be aware," and the Old German *munthen*, "to awaken." The older understanding of math described a way to awaken to and be conscious of the beautiful order and unfolding nature of the world we live in.

> # Geometry existed before creation.
>
> *—Plato*

At the academy that Plato founded in Rome, he required that his students study mathematics as a prerequisite for the study of philosophy. He believed that numbers were the highest degree of knowledge, that they were actually knowledge themselves, and that to learn them was to learn the foundation of wisdom and reality. Numbers and patterns brought self-awareness through an awareness of the original language of our universe. This profound understanding of numbers as knowledge was well integrated into art, religion, philosophy, technology, and everyday life of ancient Greece. Likewise, when I create shapes, patterns, and symmetry, I do so with the understanding that I am truly creating with the symbolic language of the universe that expresses itself in harmony and balance. And that language brings harmony and balance to my own life as well.

Most importantly, play! Play with flowers, berries, and bark. Be a child. Create shapes that please your eye and open your heart. Know that the shapes you make and the patterns you form through those shapes are speaking to you of something quite profound. And perhaps, through playing with these patterns, you might come across something simple and yet profound about your own purpose and your place in this infinite cosmic rippling.

Let Beauty Be Your Language

I'll tell you a secret: When I create, I talk to myself. Well, not just to myself but also to everything around me.

"The pinecone looks amazing in the center. Yes! I love you there." *"How about those dark red berries? Do you gals want to play with the pinecone?"* <carefully puts down 30 berries in a circle around the pinecone> *"Nah, I don't like it like that."* <carefully picks up the 30 berries> *"How about those dried leathery-looking leaves I found? Do you guys have something to say?"*

And it goes on like this. This is a conversation. A negotiation of trying things out. Doing and adjusting. And the key is to listen. From the way I see it, everything is speaking, either to me or to each other. My function is to learn the language.

Sometimes it takes hours. There was a time-lapse video made of me building an altar recently. The assumption was that it would be a brief video showing my process from start to finish. I was working with vertebrae, stone, and handsome jet-black crow feathers I found on the side of the road. But for the life of me, I could not understand how to get these items to speak to each other. It seemed like distinctly stubborn voices were speaking over each other, which made for some very slow progress. Throughout the video, you can watch my persistent attempts to bring them into a dialogue of harmony, where it doesn't look like separate voices all competing to be heard but one evolving conversation.

My purpose is to keep the pieces speaking to each other, even if I continue to change their placement. The name of the game is to find a common language that will allow the separate parts to speak to each other synergisti-

cally. With that particular altar, those pieces didn't want to come together until half an hour before sundown. And then, bam, they harmonized in one voice.

This past summer I was commissioned to build an altar for the city of Moab, Utah. The placement of the altar was to be under a tree that was ripe with these bright and beautiful tiny orange berries. I noticed that many berries had dropped already. In the hot desert sun, some of those older fallen berries had dried into a gorgeously dark burnt orange while others had hardened into an aged pomegranate-like color. When I held all the different combinations of the same berry in my hand, they spoke to me in harmonic chords. I realized that they complemented each other quite exquisitely. As I placed them on the altar, I was taken with the way these old and new sunsoaked berries played with each other. While I was creating with them, they were the ones guiding me and I was learning their language.

Learning the language of arrangement asks you to pay attention to what is already there. The incredible aerodynamic curve of the seagull feather can inform you how it wants to be placed. Try it out. Hold one in your hand and slowly lower it to the ground. Most likely, the feather has a side it prefers to lay on. When I build altars with feathers, or anything for that matter, I don't resist their preferences, I obey them. I look to see if their natural shape and expression complements another. Does the curve of the feather agree with the curve of the magnolia leaf? And maybe they don't agree, which is

fine, but in their disagreement they could create an entirely new conversation and, frankly, I find that incredibly exciting. I'm always listening for a new conversation to emerge.

Right behind the cabin where I am writing, a team of stonemasons is building a stone wall against the side of the hill. While talking with them about their work, they shared with me "the way of the rock," which is a practice of bringing the rocks together in conversation with each other. They told me that you can't force two rocks together. The rock itself will dictate to you where it wants to go, and it is their job to listen to that and chisel away parts of it to help it fit there. These masons were consistently learning how to let a rock be itself, and part of their job was to be patient and learn about each stone. As much as they might try to develop a plan for how many feet of wall they want to build that day, the rocks require them to put aside their expectations of how they think things should be for the sake of the greater conversation of the whole rock wall. Apparently, you can't force them to come together, because if you try to do that they'll break.

One mason told me that when he first started as a mason, he spent almost an entire day trying to fit one rock into one spot. As many times as he tried, it would not fit because he didn't yet understand the "zen of rocks." He said he was being tested to let go of the way he wanted things to be and to listen to how the actual rock wanted to fit. He looked around at his coworkers who were placing rocks seamlessly, and he felt discouraged. After really considering what wasn't working, he

realized that he was trying to force the rock without taking the time to read it and consult with it. He hadn't yet learned their language and allowed the conversation to unfold naturally, so he changed his approach and began to listen to the stones.

Conversations need space to come into themselves. We must let them meander and evolve. We must let the stories and meanings come forward on their own. All too often we force a conversation along, hurrying it up to get to the point. We demand it go somewhere specific due to time or money constraints or because we're trying to figure something out. I'm reminded again of the conversation with the stonemasons. The masons shared with me that when they felt winter coming on, it made them stressed. They tried to push themselves to move faster and harder, which actually had the opposite effect and made the work more challenging. They recognized that a compromise was in order. And so they worked with steady persistence due to their deadlines, but in a mindful way that did not rush the work or force their conversation with the stones. It seemed like the masons were finding that right balance of giving their work some space but not too much.

So how do we step out of our own need to control a situation and to learn the language of negotiation? How do we bring together what we're looking for and what the other is also wanting itself? How do we both represent our vision, desire, and goals as well as to let go and really hear what else is wanted? Whether it's building a wall or an earth altar, there's a balance at hand between directing and being directed—of seeing how things should go and really letting the pieces inform us of how they want to fit. There's a dynamic flexibility inherent in that approach. We so desperately need to bring this way of

conversing to all our relationships. Working with the Earth is one of the best ways to attune ourselves to this method of conversation. And perhaps, through that collaborative dialogue, we can really bring something beautiful into this world.

Limitations Are Crucial

I think I don't like them. At times, I'm convinced they are unnecessary. I keep trying to push past through them. But when it comes down to it, limitations are the reason my art and expression exist at all. When working in nature, I'm faced with them at every turn—the limitation of light, the limitation of time, the limitation of materials, the limitation of life—and somehow I have to create in their midst. Every altar I have ever made was not free from but rather was informed by the very limitations of the moment I was creating within: The flower is shriveling, the sun is setting, the wind is blowing, the rain is starting, and with that, I create. My purpose as a creator and arranger is to utilize those limitations and to learn how to create from them—at the edge of them even. Creations born from limitations are a recipe for magic.

Some of the most glorious creations in this world have come from the most limited of circumstances. Beethoven composed many of his masterpieces without his ability to hear. Grant Achatz, the chef of the famous Chicagoan restaurant, Alinea, was diagnosed with cancer of the tongue and had to cook without the use of his taste buds. Hanging in the very room where I am writing there are several gorgeous paintings of intricately designed portraits and landscapes painted by a quadriplegic sixteen-year-old who used her mouth instead of her hands. What is possible in the presence of what limits us is miraculous. It takes a certain devotion to persist and pursue an endeavor when faced with limitations, because those very limitations help us recognize what we must bring into this world.

But this point of view is not championed by the culture we live in. Rather, we are taught to value the limitless—that the more we have the better. Freedom and unlimited potential are the national myths that become individual aspirations. Endless growth is our nation's economic goal. There's an expectation that we should always have what we want and have more than we need. We like our grocery store shelves stocked with 50 different types of cereal and our customer service available 24/7. We subscribe to thousands of cable channels that we can get lost in while trying to find something to watch, and we expect online services to deliver whatever we want whenever we want it. Sure, more options, more availability, and more possibility sound great—but I challenge you to ask yourself what goes missing when you only seek the unlimited?

Here's an idea: Limitations are what create value. Limitations give us an understanding of the preciousness of what we have. They remind us that nothing lasts forever. They interrupt variety and help us get clear with what matters and where our priorities lay. They humble us even as they encourage us not to collapse in their midst, and maybe even persist because of them. With too much abundance, too much variety, and an unlimited amount of time, we can get lazy, indecisive, and take things for granted. Limitations challenge us to employ our human ingenuity, make decisions, and become better with less. They also fuel creativity.

As you can tell from my art, I can be quite the perfectionist, fixating on preciseness and exactness. I will lie down on the earth, with my eyes parallel to the ground, so I can be sure that all the berries align with the eucalyptus bark just as I want them to. I will attempt to make the asym-

> Limitations are a necessary partner in the creative act as well as in the crafting of a successful life.
> —*Anne Bogart*

metrical symmetrical and the imbalanced balanced. I find a deep satisfaction with that. I strive to push the limits of the way I express myself and the way I order and arrange nature. It is a healthy expression for my mind. But I need limitations to keep me from becoming so obsessed with the details that I forget the larger process.

I often say that if I created my art indoors—with endless access to light and no wind to contend with—I would never finish. Making art outside forces my perfectionism to exist inside a reality bigger than itself. The altar I created this morning, for instance, felt utterly incomplete when I had to stop. But this was beyond my control. It's mid-December and the light starts to wane at about 3 PM. Choices had to be made so that I could finish while there was still enough light, and yet I still wanted more time. At this time of the year, this is my ongoing plea with the sun: "More time, it's not done, there's more to do, one more thing, not yet, more time, please, pleaaaaase." Thankfully, the sun did not obey my childlike petition. It continued onward and I was forced to come up against incompletion. This is never easy but it is sometimes necessary. In this way, my perfectionist gets to find beauty in the imperfection. There is always a desire for more, and as an artist this desire is relentless. But the limitation lets me learn how and when to say "good enough."

As Above, So Below

In the spring of 2016, my Orphan Wisdom School cohort and I gathered for the last time on Cortez Island in Canada for our final class. For months beforehand, we

had been crafting a collective gift to give our teacher, Stephen Jenkinson, and his beloved wife, Nathalie, which was a large quilt handmade by our entire class. Stitched over many months and with many hands, the quilt was filled with seventy-two squares, each square contained eight triangles inside of it, which looked like a little pinwheel. Each student was asked to create their own square using the same pattern, but we were also given the freedom to select our own unique fabric choices. And what an array of crazy and colorful fabrics they were! When sewed together, each square next to each square, all those little pinwheels created a pattern of circles within circles and diamonds within diamonds. We unveiled the quilt and the whole thing came alive as a kaleidoscopic image of shapes connecting to each other. Each of our separate squares, when arranged and sewed together, harmonized into this beautiful handmade quilt that was an expression and gift of many into one.

LIMITATION EXERCISE

While you might think springtime is my favorite season to build altars, because so many plants are blossoming and there is such an explosion of color bursting everywhere, this wouldn't be true. I actually love winter—always have, always will. I love the sparseness and silence it brings. As an earth artist, winter challenges me by providing such a limited palette to work with. It asks me to let what is here be enough. To create something from very little is a practice that brings forth hidden beauty in ways you would never think possible.

So here is my challenge to you, should you choose to accept it:

Make an altar only using *three* sources of material. Use as much of that material as you wish, but limit your altar to a palette of three.

Yes, three.

Perhaps this may initially be frustrating, considering how much is available to us all the time and how addicted we are to options, but see if you can find liberation in the limitation. The times I have worked with a limited palette have taught me to be innovative, crafty, and incredibly imaginative. Some of the most favorite altars I have ever made contained only one or two material sources.

One of my favorite television shows is *Project Runway*. I absolutely love the way the competition takes incredibly talented fashion designers and puts them in extremely limiting circumstances. Some of the challenges require the contestants to innovate and make high-end fashion with trash, pool toys, or even candy. They always are given a limited budget and a grueling time constraint. While all the designers would prefer different circumstances, the competition pushes them to locate their creativity in places they never would have thought possible. And, very often, they surprise themselves and create designs that push the boundaries of their imagination.

So surprise yourself. Make an altar with limited material and let that limitation feed your creativity.

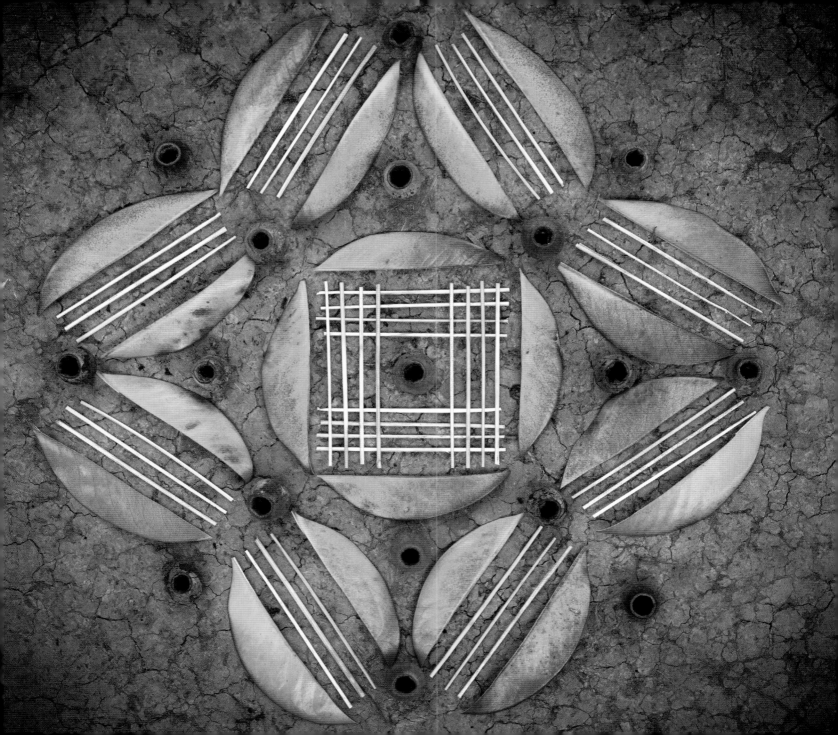

This is what you and I are doing as well: bringing many into one is the pinnacle of our Morning Altars practice. Through your hands and imagination, you have the capacity to arrange many seemingly distinct and different pieces into a collaboration of togetherness. When you do that, you are fulfilling a larger purpose in life, for life itself is always striving to come together again and again to make some order of itself. When we look at the smallest subatomic particles and the largest galaxy clusters, we can see they are doing that too. The same is true for snowflakes, crystals, plants, fruits, weather patterns, and even our bodies. No matter if we look more closely or from great distances, we can see that life expresses itself in cycles and patterns! Perhaps to our distracted and busy human eye these objects may look disconnected and unintegrated, but that's actually not the case. Nature is a living collection of small patterns evolving into larger ones.

Now maybe you're asking, how is this relevant to me and my life? Well, consider this: You are part of the universe, intricately connected to it and tied together with it. You are not an isolated person, separate and abandoned from a larger purpose in life. Heck no! You are a child of the universe who yearns to find all the infinite ways she is connected and woven into the patterns of life. Look smaller and see bigger! As is above, so is below! Proof of your connectedness exists all around you. But don't take my word for it—try creating it with your hands.

When we practice building our altar and bring many pieces of nature's treasures into one impermanent piece of art, we are aligning ourselves with life's harmonic movement. Whatever we arrange on the earth is a beautiful reminder that our natural state of being human longs to connect and be connected to everything. In all of the

THE BASICS:
Creating

Take any item from your foraged basket or bag and place it in the center.

Start in the center and just keep rippling out from there, placing new objects down.

The most important thing you can do is to play and experiment.

Try out different shapes—triangles, squares, circles, and spirals.

See if different shapes want to repeat into patterns.

Give yourself a limit, because patterns can continue indefinitely.

Your entire altar then is a mirror of the universe, many patterns into one beautiful whole.

ways we think we are different, are also all the ways we are intricately tied together. We can see this all over. Be it in quilts, beehives, Morning Altars, or Islamic tilings, these patterns let us access a feeling of deep, whole peace. The feeling we get from these geometric patterns weaves us back into a recognition of oneness and connection. It reminds us of the greater collective story we

are a part of: that all the infinite ways the many in life are becoming one.

Even the origin of the words we use illustrate this cosmic story. The word *cosmos* is commonly defined as "the universe" or "outer space"; but etymologically, the word is a Latinized form of the Greek word *kosmos,* meaning "good order or orderly arrangement." It suggests that while the universe itself is made of infinite stars, planets, and galaxies stretching out forever into space, it is really a pattern within a pattern, a harmonic and holy ordering of itself. The word *cosmetics* carries the same implications, and while we may understand it to mean lipstick, blush, and mascara, it comes from the same root as *cosmos* and more rightly refers to the act of adorning and arranging the face in harmony with itself. Beauty making is a way to make many things whole.

Sometimes, and especially today, with so many pieces fractured and so many people fractioned, we need to find our way back to wholeness and belonging. Adorning life by bringing forth these patterns and symmetry is a way we can do that. Creating a Morning Altar, just like basket making, knitting, masonry, braiding, and cooking, is just another way of remembering how to weave the many into one. It is through those daily hands-on practices that we remember how to come back together again—with our bodies, with our Earth, with our neighbors, with our enemies, with our creative spirit, and with the larger unfolding mystery we exist in. Life is doing this all the time all around us. If we can learn how to see it, to see the ways in which it is all connecting, and participate in it as well, we too can remember life's purpose, which is to bring that purpose into harmony with itself. Even the word *remember* means to bring different parts back together again.

So, what if this beautiful and creative expression of yours, this simple impermanent earth altar, was life arranging through you? And what if the beauty you made from many foraged objects from all over your very neighborhood was actually a gift to make life whole again? What if?

GIFT

Everybody needs beauty as well as bread, places to play in and pray in, where nature may heal and give strength to body and soul alike.

—*John Muir*

A Feast of Beauty

Imagine that you are preparing a feast. Perhaps it's a feast to feed a great many people, for a holiday or homecoming of sorts, where everyone is all gathered around one long table. Or maybe it's just an elegant candlelit dinner prepared especially for your beloved. You spend hours upon hours cooking up a storm with pots boiling, spices flavoring, meat marinating, rice steaming, and vegetables sautéing. The aroma swirling in the kitchen is quite enchanting and sends anyone nearby into a salivating dream state. The tablecloth is pressed and spread. Your best dishes are beautifully set and the ambience is charged with a kind of hospitality that would disarm and invite in the most hesitant of guests. While you plan on enjoying the food, it is the feeding that feeds your soul. This feast is a gift of love and nourishment for your guests, and their delight is yours. Serving them the food you prepared is how you transfer that love, and they receive that love when they devour the food. A gift, such as this, is given by serving it up and giving it over—letting the feast be feasted upon.

So too is your altar a feast. You've collected your ingredients, cleared the table, cooked the meal, and plated the food. The beauty that your hands have made is prepared and laid out before you. But you can't stop here. This beauty (food) must be fed in order for it to have any purpose at all. And how do you feed beauty to others? Your altar is a gift to be given and an offering to be offered up.

In the same way that the trees, plants, animals, and minerals have given generously of themselves to you, so too must your altar be an offering back to that generosity. Gifting is reciprocal, and what makes this an altar is that it carries your intention to give, bless, wish, and pray. With your intention, the beauty becomes nourishment to feed all that has fed you. Creating a Morning Altar is about understanding how much you've been on the receiving end of the gift of life and demonstrating that you do not take that gift for granted. Your hands and heart have created a beautiful gift to give back to this life so that it can continue on. This is how meaning is made.

The fifth movement of our practice is to bestow your creation as a gift. This can be done through words, song, or in silence. Regardless, the meaning is made when you give the gift over. As you may remember from the previous chapter, I spoke of rippling, which is the movement within your altar that originates in the center and expands out from there. Well, letting this altar become a gift is to allow its ripples to continue outward even more, beyond you but including you. Gifting your altar is to deeply consider all those who make up your life, seen and unseen, known and unknown, living and dead, and to let this beauty nourish them as well. It is to invite in all those who you want to see fed and cared for as you offer them this beautiful feast too.

How does the altar become a gift? A gift becomes a gift when it is given. So the question becomes, to whom or what is your beauty prepared for? Perhaps it's to honor a milestone like an anniversary or a new job, or it's an expression of the grief from a breakup, or maybe it contains a prayer for a sick mother, or maybe it's simply a celebration of another day of being alive. Whatever the reason, this is the time to name it. Let your words be the way this gift can find its recipient. Let your words be as beautiful as the altar you made. Eloquence too is food that can nourish deeply.

Also, this feast is a gift to the very land itself. Wherever you are, you have adorned this land with beauty that nourishes the Earth herself. We modern humans have forgotten that the land is not just another commodity to take from but is alive with spirit and needs to be tended and fed as well. We are constantly taking from the places where we are, but in what ways can we give back? What does it take to nourish a place that nourishes us? Well, perhaps beauty is a way we can feed a place, just as that beauty feeds our own hearts.

And then, once again, we can learn how to live generously if we give daily. We humans once understood that as a way of life. We once walked around on this abundant Earth more aware of the mysterious and not so mysterious ways of being given to, fed, tended, and cared for. We understood the indebtedness that we owed the land, the animals, our neighbors, our family, and the spirit that gave us and continues to give us our life. Offering gifts every day was a way to acknowledge these constant gifts and to feed them to others so that they could continue to be given.

So now we give over our beauty that we made. We offer our altar to something or someone bigger than ourselves and perhaps to a part of ourselves that needs nourishment too. But most important is to practice making it a gift by giving it. Ring that bell, invite over your beloveds, and serve up that feast!

The Gift Flows

Before I explain the process of offering your altar as a gift to be given back to all the remembered and forgotten parts that constitute your life, please allow me to speak about the process of gifting in general, for it is truly an old and elegant art form. I believe if we can understand the purpose of a gift, especially a handmade one, how it moves, and what our responsibilities are to it, then the gifting of our altars can be even more resonant.

As I write this, it happens to be Christmas Day. It is an apropos time to be writing a chapter on giving and gifting. People all over the world are waking up today having just spent the past month tirelessly preparing, shopping, and purchasing gifts for their family and friends. Probably at this very moment those presents are piled up under twinkling Christmas trees, wrapped in soon-to-be torn-up paper, and awaiting all those good boys and girls who they are meant for. So much of December is devoted to the spirit of giving, but in our culture, a culture of commodities, what underlies this month of giving is a month of buying. So many of the gifts sitting under those trees, or in my case, under that menorah, were bought in stores and wrapped as gifts. I remember while growing up in suburban New York, every Chanukah night we would go through the ritual of lighting the candles and singing the old songs, but what I really waited for was that new Nintendo game or Cabbage Patch Kids doll. The holiday was about giving, but really it was about expecting. I was raised to be constantly on the take, even and especially during a time of generosity.

Occasionally, there would be the handmade gift that my grandmother would offer, like a sweater that must have taken her hands quite some time to knit and a whole lot of time thinking of me while doing so. But honestly, that kind of gift wasn't valuable to me. The sweater was a more complex gift to receive because it brought me closer into my relationship with my grandmother, and it reminded me of her every time I wore it. At the time, I didn't understand the worth of a handmade gift, what it asked of me, and the significant difference it had as compared to a store-bought item. I was young.

For much of my life, when I bought something in a store, say a sweater, my only responsibility was to pay for it. The sweater's exchange began and ended with the exchange of money and a perfunctory remark. Nothing more was asked or expected of me and so, after paying for it, that was the end of the relationship with the seller. The author Lewis Hyde says in his book *The Gift* that "the cardinal difference between gift and commodity exchange is that a gift establishes a feeling-bond between two people, while the sale of a commodity leaves no necessary connection." So true. Buying a sweater from a store actually asks nothing more from me than my money.

But a gifted sweater is different. I have a dear friend whose recently deceased mother was a well-practiced crafter and gifter. The gifts she gave her family weren't your average gifts. They carried heft and weight because they were woven with relationships. When she learned how to knit, it wasn't enough to buy the yarn. She learned how to raise her own sheep, sheer the sheep, dye the wool, work the wool into yarn with her spindle, and knit it into beautifully made sweaters and scarves for her loved ones. The sweater carried the relationships of the animals, the land, and all those who passed on the skills of dying, spindling, and knitting. Even though my friend's mother is now deceased, her hands, her heart, all the ways she loved the world and the way she knew how to love her daughter, are all embedded in that one sweater. My friend has the privilege of receiving a gift so full of connections!

There is no better teacher of gifting and giving than our Earth. Robin Wall Kimmerer writes in *Braiding Sweetgrass* about all the gifts that the Earth gives to her life and her people, especially the sacred sweetgrass, or what is called in her native language *wiingaashk*, the sweet-smelling hair of Mother Earth. This long, braided grass is a medicine and gift given by the land to her people to honor, heal, and bless the community. Because it cannot be bought for ceremonial purposes, it carries the original intent of the gift, which is to be freely given. When the sweetgrass is burned with the ceremonial fire, it is a gift kept in motion, first given by the land to the people and then by the people back to the spirit of the community and land. She says, "Many of our ancient teachings counsel that whatever we have been given is supposed to be given away again." This reciprocal exchange, giving and receiving, or as the root of the word *reciprocity* suggests, *re* and *pro*, back and forth, is the fundamental relationship between the Earth and the people. We receive and are obligated to give back to the Earth and receive again, and so on.

Kimmerer reminds us that while most people in our consumer culture think that a gift is free, because we

> You give but little when you give of your possessions.
> It is when you give of yourself that you truly give.
>
> —*Kahlil Gibran*

obtain it at no cost, it is far from that. "In the gift economy, gifts are not free. The essence of the gift is that it creates a set of relationships. The currency of a gift economy is, at its root, reciprocity. In Western thinking, private land is understood to be a 'bundle of rights,' whereas in a gift economy property has a 'bundle of responsibilities' attached."

Because my art is made of the land, I've come to understand some of these gifting responsibilities. One morning, I was up at dawn with my dog Rudy, foraging in the hills behind my house for materials to build an altar. It was late summertime, well into the dry season, and most of those hills were filled with golden grasses, giving California its famous name, The Golden State. The milk thistle, however, was out in full bloom. It seemed to have waited for that last moment to bring forth its most incredible electric blue and purple flowers, all dripping with nectar that drove the pollinators wild. In situations like this, I am very reluctant to harvest anything still growing. It just doesn't feel right. But after sitting for a while with my resistance and just taking in the marvel of this plant and her beautiful blossoms, I shared with her my longing to make art with her glorious flower. I don't know how to explain it but to my surprise, it felt like she offered me a gift—the invitation to harvest her flowers. So in return, I offered the plant a little tobacco. According to most Native American tribes, tobacco is a unifying thread of communication between the human and spirit worlds, and it is traditionally offered either in smoke or as a dry leaf as a sign of gratitude and respect. I had some in a little pouch, and I offered a little pinch as well as some water and a song. These were my own personal ways of showing my thanks. Only then did I cut the flower. Honestly, I felt both exhilarated by the find

and extremely wary about cutting any more than one. Had this been a flower shop, I may have bought a whole bouquet of milk thistle because I'd rather have more than less options when making my art. But because the plant herself offered her flower to me, I decided to restrain myself and take only one. I understood this as a gift, and I now felt a bond between that plant and myself.

Let me be clear, I don't believe that this plant's flower blossomed so that it could be given to me. Plants are living, animate beings that belong only to themselves. I'm not entitled to her flowers. I think we have to be very discerning about how we frame our understanding of "being given" and the entitlement that surrounds that, especially in our self-centered American culture. Intention and perception here are everything. After listening and offering my intention to the plant, only then did I sense anything like permission. And because I chose to receive the flower as a gift, my relationship with this plant transformed, as did my sense of obligation toward it. I wasn't just taking something I wanted, but rather I understood it as something being given and, therefore, I had both the inspiration and the responsibility to give back. If we humans can shift our perspectives to see how much we are taking and to practice receiving with humbleness, gratitude, and obligation to give again, then we can change how we relate both to the living world around us and to each other. And this shift in perspective and behavior has enormously positive consequences. According to scholar and writer Lewis Hyde, "The return gift is, then, fertilizer that assures the fertility of the source." In other words, in a gifting economy, through giving and receiving gifts, we are a part of and not separate from the fecundity with all our relationships. It's kind of like, the more we give, the more that grows.

The poverty of our time is that we modern humans see everything as a collection of commodities that we can take without any obligation to give back. Animals, plants, and minerals are objects that are to be caged, farmed, and mined in order to feed and supply our never-satiated hunger for more. While writing this book in Southern Utah, I am doing so in the middle of a travesty in which Donald Trump and greedy Utahan Senators like Orren Hatch have removed the protection of the Escalante Staircase's monument in order to drill for uranium and coal. The level of theft and disconnection is heartbreaking, considering that this land, a living treasure, has been essentially untouched since the days of the dinosaurs. It is a travesty to sell it to the highest bidder as a commodity. How did our so-called leaders and culture get to be so removed from the natural world, a world that gives us everything we need to live and live well, that we see everything nonhuman (and sometimes, even human) as only resources to take? When did our dominant culture forget the interdependent reciprocity of life, a system we depend on, and our obligation to it?

According to Hyde's extensive scholarship, our world remains plentiful because it is given, received, and given back again as gifts. If we only show up to take and not give back, the consequences are clear. These days, those of us who are not fooling ourselves look at an Earth going through dramatic climate change. My own home this year is only an hour from a devastating fire that destroyed much of Santa Rosa, California—this fire being just one of many enormous wildfires in my home state. The more we take from our planet, the poorer and more homeless we become.

This reality of our dominant culture mining the living world for raw materials while converting us into hungry

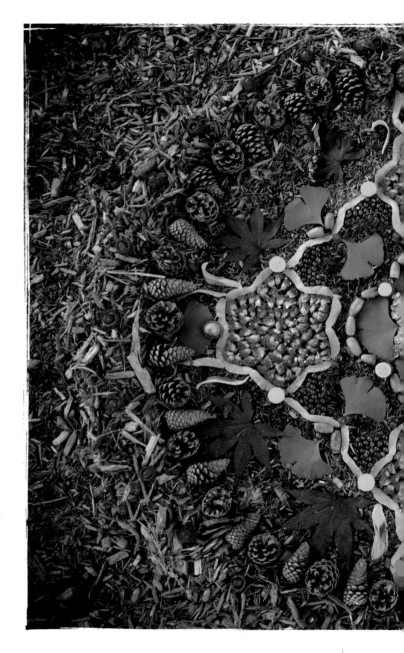

consumers has continued on for more than four hundred years. Perhaps now is the time to consider a new yet very old story—one that centers on reciprocity and responsibility. The author Charles Eisenstein, in a conversation with Oprah Winfry, challenges us to consider that "this story of separation is falling apart and the story of connection and union, the knowing of the heart, now no longer needs to conflict with our beliefs." As for the knowing of the heart, he says, "The more you give, the richer you are, which is the opposite of a money culture." The money culture has taught us that everything has a monetary value and so can be bought and sold. But the older story, known and lived by our ancestors who had an integral and reciprocal relationship with the Earth, suggests that this relationship with our living world is beyond value and beyond price. Maintaining the gift of all of our relationships was and is everything.

We are living off the gifts of all that has come before us: humans, plants, animals, and minerals. What came before us lived long enough to pass on this gift of life, and it is our obligation to keep the gift in motion for the next generations. We must remember how to wake up each day and realize that just being here today, having a family, drinking fresh water, breathing clean air, and having a home to come back to is the privilege that we're being granted. If we can see how much we're taking all the time, if we can stop to remember how many hands went into making us our food, clothing, cars—how many animals and plants have gone into giving us our medicine and homes and how many minerals have gone into our phones and computers—then maybe, just maybe, this remembering can move us to give back and to make a conscious choice to live our lives as an ever-refining, ever-moving gift that we receive and offer back to the world.

Offering the Gift

So are you seeing how this all works? Your altar is a beauty-making ritual for you to practice the Great Art of Giving. But before this, allow me to ask you a question that pleads for your consideration: What is giving you your life?

Don't answer. Witness first. Take in a breath and feel the sweet rush of air fill out those beautiful lungs. Feel the solid and living Earth underneath your body, holding and supporting you no matter how heavy the load you carry. Look at your own two hands and notice the size and shape of them, a weaving together of all your ancestors' ancestors in the wrinkles and marks on your palms. And consider all that you have and all that you've lost on this long road of your life.

Perhaps this altar is an offering to the grief of loving what you had—a home, a partner, a job, parents. Perhaps they are now gone from your sight, and the longing expressed in this altar reminds you of how much you love and miss them. Or perhaps it is offered to the love and deep appreciation of what you still have, what still walks with you through your days. Your altar reminds you not to take companionship for granted, asks you to remember that all things mysteriously come and go, and invites you to cherish and care for them as much as you can right now.

Your love for life and all you've been granted arrives to this feasting table, this Morning Altar, through your contemplation of it.

Gifting is a meditation. You've been on the receiving end of so much life, some of which you prefer and a hellava lot that you don't. But right now it's not your preferences that matter; it's your consideration—your willingness to inventory all of that which curiously gathers around your days, big and small, and to take the time to thank the heavens that you have the privilege of knowing your life in the presence of all that constitutes it. Am I talking about being grateful? Maybe, though there's more to it. It's more like praise. It's more like seeing what you've had and lost and what you still have, and praising it as a way of loving it.

A few summers ago, I witnessed a kind of praise that made it rain. That season had not actually seen rain in almost six months, and much of California's reservoirs were dangerously close to being evaporated away. I had never witnessed Wildcat Canyon so cracked and thirsty before, looking like the hands of a very old person who had been through many seasons of their life. My neighbors, friends, and even the mailman had rain on their mind in a way I had never experienced before, when living in New York. Everyone talked about it, longed for it in a way that began to sound a lot like a prayer.

That morning was overcast, a relief from the incessant heat that was unusual for summertime in the Bay Area. I set out with basket in hand and a Spotify station playing my "foraging mix" when someone tapped me on the shoulder. A man, most likely homeless, with sad, kind eyes asked me what I was doing. He seemed both shy and very curious about my purpose with the basket. Usually most people think I'm out picking herbs for tea or medicine, but this man just simply asked: "What are you doing?" I let him know that "I'm just makin' art from the land." "Art from the land?" He had never heard of such a thing and, to my surprise, asked if he could join me and possibly make something too. Why not?!

Along the way, we got to talking. He opened up a bit about his life and the struggles he had with keeping a steady job. I could tell he had some barriers built up around his heart, but it also seemed to me that he really just wanted to talk to someone. We hiked to the top of the hill and sat down together between two sister walnut trees. Before we began to build, I asked him to consider why he was building this art, that perhaps it had a greater purpose to be devoted to. In his quiet way he said he'd consider it.

We worked in silence for what must have been a couple of hours, and as I looked up from my altar, I could see this man crying. We both stared into his arrangement of walnuts, bay leaves, eucalyptus bark, and wild oat tops for some time. Eventually, through the silence and tears, he shared with me another layer of his life: that his alcohol addiction almost killed him last year and he didn't think he would live to see this summer. But for reasons both known and unknown to him, he had now been sober for almost 12 months. He showed me that in the shape of this altar. It looked like a wheel with 12 spokes, with one spoke devoted to each month of his sobriety. He explained that the first spoke of the wheel consisted of dead bark, but as it progressed, each spoke became more alive, with the last one being made entirely of green and flourishing leaves.

Through his hands and his words, this man was praising his life, both his efforts to stay sober and all the seen and unseen support that has helped him do so. He let me know that his life was not a guaranteed thing, that he had lost so much from his addiction already. And yet his altar told the story of someone who was coming back to life. I witnessed him recommit to another 12 months of sobriety, to his healing, and to serving all that had served him. His courageous words sent a shiver up my spine and brought an "amen" to my lips.

A powerful silence followed, a moment that seemed to mark time, which was abruptly interrupted by a sound I hadn't heard for quite a while—the sweet sound of rain dropping on the dry fallen leaves of the walnut tree. We both looked up and then at each other. There was great wonder and mystery in our eyes. The rain didn't last very long, maybe a minute or so, but I couldn't help but consider if this man's brokenhearted praise of his life brought the rain. In those moments, when the separation and barriers built around our hearts crumble, when we can open ourselves in grief and praise of what really matters, then perhaps that is what is needed to feed this parched earth and nourish us during these unsettling times. Whenever I pass those two sister walnut trees, I think about this devoted man and this holy moment. I remember his altar-wheel of sobriety and how his love of life and his desire to live made it rain.

Living Praise

The altar you made can make it rain too.

Maybe your altar won't bring rain from the sky, but it can bring much-needed nourishment back to all of life, yours included!

But here's the thing. This altar is only one meal, a daily ritual whose purpose is to remind you that every moment of your life can be offered up as a hand-crafted, gracefully shared, generously given, precious gift. Praise isn't something that's just spoken, it's also something that is done. Beauty and praise are made by the way you live your life, how you walk about your day, how you do business, the way you speak to your partner, the way you speak to yourself, who you share your meals with, the way you eat food and where you get it from, the gratitude you bring to your mornings or nights, the remembrance of all those here and all those gone, and your willingness to fall in love with the smallest and grandest wonders of the world. The author, teacher, and wild-man shaman, Martín Prechtel, puts it like this, "If the way we live does not praise life, then we are not alive."

I once heard the old-time English storyteller Martin Shaw say, "If you want to be fed, become bread." I've come to understand that this riddle speaks both to the hungry poverty of our times and instructs us toward our purpose. The first time I met my teacher, Stephen Jenkinson, he said something similar and I've never forgotten it. He asked, "Can you show up in your life needed instead of needy?"

My ancestors totally got this. They understood the necessity of feeding the world that was feeding them. During the reign of Solomon and David's temple in Jerusalem, people made offerings of animals, plants, and minerals on the temple's fire altar as a way to feed God with the abundance of the land. That ancient Biblical culture understood that you can't just be on the take all the time and that whatever you grew, you gladly gave part of it as a gift back to God. My ancestors practiced the reciprocal relationship of receiving and giving. All the gifts of the first crops and firstborn animals were called in Hebrew *karbanot*, which means "offerings." But this word's very root is *l'karov*, which means "to come close to"—a remembering as to what the purpose of the offering really was. In other words, that which we are offering is a way of coming closer to whatever is sacred in our lives.

So the purpose of asking you the question, "What is giving you your life?" is to remind you to make the invisible visible. Whenever I gift an altar, I take time to consider this question in silence.

I let myself linger in the presence of all that constitutes my life, all that I am privileged to be on the receiving end of. I linger long enough so that I begin to transmute that low-grade, mindless entitlement into rich awe. I am awed by my life, which really isn't mine at all. When that awareness rises up inside me and threatens to break my heart or head wide open, I channel that awe through my mouth. My words speak what my heart feels. I see these words as the last arrangement of my altar, the grace before the meal, and my humble and impossible attempt to remember where all of it came from and how insanely blessed I am to have been visited by it, even temporarily.

Practice Praising

Your depression is connected to your insolence and refusal to praise.

—Rumi

So now it's your turn to practice praising. As with the creative process, there is no right way to do so. Some days, when I'm inspired, my acknowledgment sounds a bit like poetry; while at other times, it might come across as a basic and simple thank you. However you do it, the most important thing is to speak from your heart and do so authentically. Give the gift of your efforts and imagination generously.

If praising is new to you and you're looking for more structure, consider the pebble in the pond metaphor. Let your words of devotion be like a ripple that reaches out beyond you. Maybe it sounds like a request, an ask, or a blessing that remembers and wishes for the well-being of that which you love and want to maintain in the world. This can be offered to the smallest and most for-

gotten of things that many would consider insignificant but that we couldn't live without. A friend once spent 10 minutes praising the dishes that served her family and her community. She made a point of honoring those plates, because they carried innumerable meals in times of sorrow and celebration throughout her everyday life.

Of course, you can devote your altar to the recognition of the biggest of thoughts, especially the unthinkable ones, like the nighttime sky and its infinite galaxies, or the innumerable ancestors in your lineage, names that you'll never know and stories that have been long forgotten but whose presence in the world was necessary to bring forth your life. Either way, try and let wonder lift your tongue.

I particularly like to acknowledge everything that exists in the world that I don't know and doesn't benefit me in the slightest but is good and necessary in its own right. You can even offer your altar to that which you think you love the least or that doesn't seem beautiful to you in the slightest. Doing this engages the spirit of

generosity, which is a transformative power that can alter relationships and encounters, and reminds us of what binds us together rather than separates us.

Sometimes I begin my offering with the words, "May I," "May we," or "Would it be." I do this because I truly believe that the courtesy of praise centers on asking. Praise asks us to surrender our demand and entitlement that things be exactly as we want them to be. These words remind me of my humble position as a human to make requests and ask permission of a power bigger than me. It's not my position or interest to tell you what that power is—maybe you call it God or Goddess, Spirit, Life Force, Jesus, Yahweh, Allah, Krishna, The Tao, Great Mystery, Earth Mother, Intelligent Universe, or maybe nothing at all. You know what that power is, and that's plenty fine. The point is this: Let's not assume that because we want it, we get it; rather, let us seek through asking, and let us cultivate a kind of courtesy in our offering that truly makes it into a gift.

Oftentimes I'm so humbled by what I'm attempting to speak to that I don't know how to begin. It is actually a wonderful way to begin making an offering. For example, I recently built an altar and offered it up to the generosity of those good people who invited me to stay at this ranch while I write this book, as well as the spirit of the land here. As I finished the altar, which was made of slick rocks, dried grass, piñon pinecones, and juniper berries, I saw the sun dip below the hills in the west and I was overcome with the kind of gratitude that floored me. After a time of being completely unsure of how to respond to it all, I eventually found my way to say something like, "I truly don't know where to begin. I don't know how I came to be so blessed and well cared for, that someone like me

OVERLOOKED INTIMACIES

Acknowledgment is food. Praise is food. Thanks is food. Beauty is food. Let your altar-feast inspire you to nourish all those who you know well and love, human and nonhuman, living and dead, seen and unseen, holy and mundane, and participate in the reciprocal process of receiving and giving. By doing that, you can begin to make your entire life into an altar, arranged so beautifully so as to be a gift back to feed the whole. You can practice living in praise.

Here is my little exercise to you, should you be willing: See something small and almost forgotten in your life. Even better, see something that is mundane and everyday and appreciate it. Offer your altar to all those overlooked intimacies.

could be given so much. . . ." The honest fact is that when you can truly presence even a fraction of the generosity that makes up your life and your day, being speechless and tongue-tied is actually a proper response to all you've been given. Beginning there, even with a stumbling of words, may contain all the gratitude and love that you're attempting to express. Humbleness doesn't need to be done right, it just needs to be done. Indeed, humility actually is what might be needed these days. In a culture in which we're expected to be competent and masterful at everything we do, in which we're expected to always be "on" and have it all figured out, it's a good practice to let ourselves be unsure and hesitant and speak from that place. For this is often how something unexpected and wonderful finds its way through you.

So now it's your turn to acknowledge and serve up this feast of yours by inviting all of that which you want to feed, and all of that which has fed you. Don't worry about it needing to sound a certain way. Start with not knowing. Don't sweat the feeling that you're speaking to "no one"— for perhaps something unseen is listening to you. Most important, give this moment the gift of your attention and consideration! What is giving you your life? Your obligation is to move the gift forward and help that keep existing in the world.

And that is where we can really access our praise. It is in our capacity to get so close to someone or something, to know their ways so well and to see those ways, even if they frustrate the hell out of us, because that is the way they are and how they express themselves to the world. Children do this incredibly well. They always attune themselves to the details of everything around them. Praise rides on the same frequency, and it comes from your willingness to observe and learn the intricacies.

Recently during a Fire Circle class, a fourteen-year-old teenager asked me what love was. Not a small question, let me tell you. He said he was starting to fall in love but didn't know if it was really it. I asked him about the girl he claimed to love and how much he

knew about her. I asked him to name the dessert she liked the most or the time of the day she prefers to read a book and what particular book she was into right now. I wondered with him about what her worries were and if he knew what kept her up at night. Patiently learning all the infinite number of ways this girl loved, lived, learned, and struggled was how I told him he would find his way toward loving her. And by seeing what it is she loved, in all its particular details, and maybe even learning how to give some of it to her so that she would have more of what she loved in this world, well, that was a way of understanding love.

Praise is love. And praise is found in the ten million details of that which you love.

So start small—tiny even.

Begin by giving a toast to all that is overlooked and forgotten.

Last night I spontaneously praised someone precious to me.

My best friend was cleaning out his text messages and sent me a bunch of videos of my dog Rudy that he had collected throughout the years. Rudy died this past April, and the hole she left in my life is wide and deep. I felt this emptiness in most hours of my day, and especially on those morning walks. And so I cherished these ridiculously adorable videos that captured her in those everyday moments of eating treats in the car, getting petted, running at the park, post-shower towel snuggles, and even one of her "I'm not walking anymore" stubborn moments for which she was quite famous. But honestly, the tears came readily when I remembered the littlest of things

about her, all those overlooked or ignored details that made Rudy Rudy: the way her little eyebrows grew in long broad wisps, and how they would stand straight up after putting her head out the car window; how she would nervously shake during her baths, when the only thing that would remotely calm her down was my slightly off-tune rendition of "Edelweiss" from *The Sound of Music*; and the way she would run along the edge of the ocean, galloping with both front paws lifting at once, looking just like a little deer as she played back and forth with the waves. My love for Rudy is found in the details of how she was and what she loved.

Marking Time

In addition to offering your altar as a gift to the Earth, to your ancestors, to your friends, and so on, you can also offer your altar to time. Yes, time.

Let me explain.

My father died in 2011. He was sixty-two years old. I remember him every day. His photos hang on the wall of my home, his guitar sits in the stand he gave me, and my voice, especially when I'm clearing my throat, makes it sound like he's actually in the room. There are times in the year when his family and friends collectively try to remember him: his birthday, his *yortzeit* (death date), and my parents' anniversary, just to name a couple. When those days arrive, it seems that the options of how to tangibly remember him are extremely limited. Those who were close to him may light a candle or say a prayer. Perhaps some of his friends will mention his name on Facebook and others who see the post will give him a thought as they go about their day. Yet, none of these ways take

too much time nor do they ask much from those who are doing the remembering. The consequence is that, over time, we do less and remember less of my dad.

As modern life speeds up, we are losing our ability to slow down and make meaning with our days. We are not taking the time to respond well and beautifully to the moments of our lives and to all that needs to be remembered. It seems like we are forgetting how to properly mark time, which is really how we make meaning with the ongoing cycles of our lives. With regard to my dad, the issue isn't that his friends and family don't want to acknowledge his memory throughout the year—I believe that they just don't know *how* to.

Marking time is ritual. It weaves us into a deeper, older, greater memory that reminds us of why we're here and what we're here for. Is it enough to just share a memory on Facebook as our outlet to remember our lives and honor them? I say no! Milestones, anniversaries, and everyday moments need more from us. They need to be acknowledged, remembered, and made as a gift given back to time.

Every single person reading this book has had ancestors, not too long ago and perhaps even still, who knew how to make things as a way of marking time, giving gratitude, and remembering. Candles were dripped, blankets woven, food prepared, wreaths constructed, clothing sewn, songs written, homes built, and all for certain reasons. Perhaps it was a death, a birth, an initiation, a holy day, a homecoming, a peace-making between families, or even the tooth fairy giving a gift for the monumental loss of a front tooth. Things were handcrafted and ritually offered as a way to acknowledge what was occurring, and it was the made-thing that carried the meaning of that moment. I know a grandmother who crochets the most

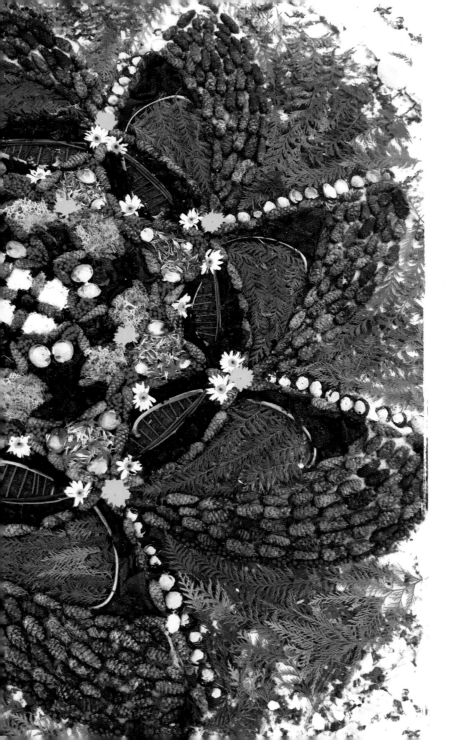

adorable baby blankets for the birth of each of her grand-children. This is her way of acknowledging that moment as a gift to be given back to the baby. Lewis Hyde calls these "gifts of passage" and their purpose is to accompany, protect, honor, and beautify those times of change.

Last year, an entire community and I built a gift of passage for a wedding on Salt Spring Island, Canada, during a remarkable blizzard. The entire island was blanketed by huge white flakes. According to the locals, it hadn't snowed like that in years. The roads were undriveable and the cedars hung low from the weight of the snow. If you had nowhere to go, which was true for many of us, it was a magical wonderland suited to welcome a bride and groom.

I knew in advance that I wanted to build an altar to mark this special event, and that I wanted it to be built by many of the guests as well. It was to become a special communal gift, born on the day of the wedding and built by the very hands of almost all of those attending. I love gifts like this. They are so rare and magical because they are an expression of the entire wedding, the nexus of beauty where the people, time, and land all meet.

Before the storm hit, a bunch of us went foraging at the shore for materials. From the sea, we collected mussel shells, different kinds of seaweed, and white sand. We also gathered up other materials like cedar leaf and pinecones from the trees surrounding the place where the ceremony was to be held. With impeccable timing, as I laid down the first few shells, the snow began to fall. And it didn't stop for days. Into the night and the following morning, our frigid hands arranged this beauty that came to look like an enormous colorful propeller spinning in the snow. Children were filling in shapes with seaweed as adults were putting shells in cascading order.

It was a fun, village-making experience. It was a gift crafted by the gathered community to mark and make the sanctity of the day.

As the bride and her bridesmaids arrived, they spontaneously circled the altar many times, walking in the same direction that the propeller was spinning, before entering the ceremonial tent. Then the entire wedding party followed suit, circling and circling the altar as it snowed, taking in the color, textures, and beauty of the art collected from the land and made from our very hands. As we circled, inspired by the beauty that was already on the ground, prayers were offered and songs were sung. It was a moment of great beauty, and it was a remarkable way to enter a ceremony in the snow.

That wedding altar still lives in that very spot. Four full seasons have passed, and it looks nothing like it did when we first made it. Grasses have grown from under it, people and animals have walked on it, and children have added things to it and probably taken from it as well. I recently received photographs a year later of children bringing flowers to remake the altar and mark the wedding anniversary. That spot is still changing but it continues to carry the memory of that day, of that storm and those of us gathered by it, as a witness that marks the union of two of our own. The beauty made was a gift from and a gift for that moment in time.

Earth altars, like all well-intentioned gifts that take time to be made, have a special capacity to mark time. The particular moment of its making, like that wedding snowstorm, becomes inseparable from the very gift itself. The time it was made in and the gift itself become one. This particular earth altar is a culminated expression of the weather, the land, the guests, and the story of all that hap-

pened that day, including the very snowy footprints of all those who circled the altar. The gift becomes a living expression of that time and carries its memory. Similarly, while those baby blankets made by that grandmother are not used anymore, they are still kept and treasured by her grandson. Their invaluableness to him is connected to the time and intention in which they were made and given, which was the threshold of his birth. The blanket gifts remind him of and binds him to that time.

For fifteen years I have been marking each birthday with an earth altar. I spend the entire day of my birthday out wandering wherever I am. If I'm in New York, I go into Central Park. If I'm in California, I go into the hills of Wildcat Canyon. I like having the time outside

to slow down, and I let the day become one of collection and reflection. Rather than just being a passive participant on my birthday, I utilize the day to remember the past year and to wonder and pray into the upcoming year. But I don't just do this in my mind—I do this with my feet and with my hands. As I arrange my birthday altar, it becomes an expression of that year of my life. It is a beautiful gift that I give back to all those who make my life possible. Then, in the evening of my birthday, I give this gift to all my friends as we all gather around it to celebrate, pour drinks, give blessings, tell stories of the past year, and, especially, give thanks for the existence of our friendship. By the end of the evening, the altar is glowing and so are we. So the point is, my birthday isn't just about me receiving gifts. It is a time of giving as well.

> By marking time with beauty made from our hands and our words, we can slow down the moment so as to find our way back into it.

Whatever the occasion, beauty can be made and given as a way that connects us back to the cycles of our life, which are always changing. If we don't mark

MILESTONE EXERCISE

Make an altar for a life event. For instance, I recently received a photo of an altar from someone in Ohio who made one to mark her graduation from university.

Make an altar for a time of the year. Consider when the equinox or solstice is, and then mark and honor the season and all that is yet to come and all that has come to pass.

Make an altar to mark something you just started or just finished. Whether it's the completion of a project at work or the first day of a long-awaited vacation, bring in or send out that moment with beauty!

these changes and honor them, they pass us by and, eventually, life passes us by entirely. Marking time is like a dancer counting the beats of music: 1, 2, 3, 4, 1, 2, 3, 4. Counting the beats is how dancers find their place inside the music. We are no different. Life is our music. And we are always trying to find our place and purpose inside of it. But to do that, we must mark our time, like the dancer. Ritual is how we do that, how we find our rhythm again in the rapid and ever-changing flow of time. It is where forgotten memory is remembered again and how the current time is reconnected to the greater cycles of time.

THE BASICS:
Gifting

Now for the beautiful words.
Your art and altar is meant to be blessed
and gifted.
Consider it a meditation where you get to
ask yourself:
Who or what am I offering this beauty to?
Or what moment am I honoring or
remembering?
This is a form of praise.
Consider starting off your words with
"May I?" or "May we?"
Practice offering your altar not only to the
biggest blessings in your life
but also the smallest and most forgotten.
If your altar is a feast, you are feeding all
that has fed you.

Chapter 6

SHARE

Why ask art into a life at all, if not to be
transformed and enlarged by its presence
and mysterious means?. . .
And by changing selves, one by one,
art changes also the outer world that
selves create and share.

—*Jane Hirshfield*

A Fierce Trust

I have made thousands of altars. And not one of them exist anymore. Each one has returned to the earth, blown away with the wind or eaten by some creature with little paws that went out foraging for a midnight snack. Sometimes they disappear immediately, like a Houdini magic trick, where hours of intense focus and impeccably placed symmetry is blown away with the single gust of a wild wind. Sometimes they decay slowly, like a long goodbye that fades over time and leaves a faint trace of what they once were. But no matter what, they all are gone.

The only thing that remains is a photograph, an instantly captured image made of pixels and megabytes, of the moment that altar was at its peak of health and vitality. This image is a memory, a husk of a fruit that once was and yet still somehow conjures the fleeting flavors of that fruit. The photograph is the evidence that these altars existed amidst a landscape of impermanence. Although photographs tell only a fraction of the story of what occurred, and can't communicate in the language of happening but only of what happened, they still have a crucial purpose. Not only do they document my work but they are also made to travel, like a seed, ready to sprout in the imagination of another person, reminding them of a timeless, mythical, and meaningful conversation of the soul.

This chapter is devoted to the sixth movement of your Morning Altars practice, which is to let your altar, process, and prayer be seen by someone other than you—your friends, family, community, and beyond. Whether you share your creation in the universe of social media or intimately with a good friend, the purpose of this

movement is for your Morning Altar to be witnessed and shared, in service to inspiring someone else. That way the gift keeps rippling out.

Oftentimes, right before you share your creativity, you might experience a great and dreaded fear that your expression won't be received well. Sometimes this fear can overpower you, so much so that instead of crossing that threshold of fear, you hold your creativity inside, keeping your expressions private, personal, and sup- pressed. Yet during these moments of fear, you must cultivate what Elizabeth Gilbert calls "a fierce trust" that says, regardless of the outcome, both you and your creations are worthy to be received. Moreover, we have no idea how our creation will impact and inspire others. The reach of our work is often far beyond our ability to know. Sometimes with that fierce trust comes an even fiercer surprise that what you made inspired another and so lives on beyond you.

ALTARS NARRATIVE

Every altar I make gets a birth certificate. Because each piece is so rooted to the time and place it was made, I use a simple structure to help me remember that time and to document that particular piece of art. I wanted to share that structure here in case you are inspired to document in a similar fashion.

Name—I love giving my altar a name. Some of them sound mythical, others are informed by the season, and others are lines taken from my favorite poems. Naming your altar gives it a way to tell its story.

Location and Season—Very important. Your altars tell of a particular place at a particular time of the year. When you record this, you are remembering your altar's connection with that moment.

Made From—This section has taught me so much about identifying plants and animals. Don't just call it a leaf, but investigate the name of the tree it came from. List all your collaborators here.

Process and Story—Tell a few sentences (or more) about your experience that day. What was the weather like? What mood were you in? What inspired you to create an altar in the first place? Invite us (or even yourself) into the experience and intention from that day.

Blessing—Start with "May I?" or "May we?" (or any other way you'd prefer) that offers the altar with a heartfelt purpose. I like to ask myself a simple question: What is this altar reminding me, or us, of that needs to be remembered, especially right now?

To Share or Not to Share

I almost didn't write this chapter.

Many people warned me not to.

They asked how a process that is so much a living and changing conversation between the land's imagination and my own, a process that is entirely organic, responsive, relational, and ephemeral could be confined and captured in a photograph. Wasn't doing so an act of removing it from the time and place it was made in?

They had more questions: Why photograph it at all? Doesn't that change the nature of what it really is and in some ways transcend its impermanence? Why not just make it and let it be, even if no other human gets to see it?

They said, Who are the altars for anyway? Are they for you? For the moment? For the land? Or are they for your fans on Instagram? Doesn't it change the way you create

if you're doing it for "likes" rather than because you're moved and inspired?

To share or not to share, that is the question.

And this is the question I want to raise to you, for if we don't question this step of the process, if we don't at least hold it up to the light and wonder about the real purpose of photographing and sharing your altar, then we can so easily lose track of the meaning that is threaded throughout your Morning Altars practice. Once again, our intention here is everything.

These days, so many of us can't experience any beautiful moments without trying to capture them on our phones and immediately post them on social media. We have become hoarders of moments, collecting them rather than living them. We've removed ourselves from the intimacy of that experience and trade it in for the immediacy of the "like." And rather than finding ourselves in the world, we try and create a world of ourselves.

Don't get me wrong, I am plenty guilty too. I struggle to not take out my phone during an epic hike or a fabulous dinner. More often than I like to admit, I fail. I attempt to capture the beauty and share it because I want everyone to know how much I've enjoyed it, and I want them to enjoy it as well. But the problem arises when I supplant my experience of the moment with the capturing of it. When getting the photograph eclipses my attentiveness toward what is happening, what is living and changing in that moment, then it is as if I wasn't even there in the first place. And when the value of that experience is measured in "likes," and the fundamental intention of sharing that photograph is to seek approval, then the real troubling question is this: Am I serving others by sharing this or am I really just serving myself?

Perhaps the question isn't to share or not to share our

Morning Altars. Rather, the question seems to be one of intention: What is the reason for sharing?

The singer Nina Simone said, "An artist's duty, as far as I'm concerned, is to reflect the times." And so it seems that with so much ugliness out there in the world, so much disempowerment and reasons to believe that our contribution doesn't matter, and with so many reasons to lose faith in our humanity and in our future, the necessity in these desperate times is in our willingness to share more beauty with each other.

Recently, I got a pack of little "compliment cards" that have 56 different deep and funny compliments written on them. From, "Those jeans make your butt look good" to "Your smile just renewed my faith in humanity," they

> A work of art is good if it has sprung from necessity.
> —*Rainer Maria Rilke*

are meant to uplift people's days. I've been secretly leaving them on seats in the subway car, on restaurant tables, and in the jacket pockets of my friends. I'm doing this because I really feel like these times are pleading for us to meet each other more generously and more kindly.

And this is why I share Morning Altars too. Far beyond my own need for "likes" or attention, I want my art to bring people back to what matters. I share because I want to celebrate the simple delights, the forgotten marvels, and the whispered reminders during these complex and burdensome times. I share because maybe, just maybe, someone will be tempted out of the trance of their glowing screens and back outside into the wild, wonderful wilderness that has given birth to us and still welcomes us back, even when we have forgotten her. I share because I want to awaken the creativity of every human being, which for too many has gone dormant in their waking lives, and to remind them that this creativity is their birthright that has been entrusted to them for a time such as this. I share because no matter what is happening in my life, the worries of my day or the stress of my budget, I long to connect my heart to everyone else and to believe beauty is magic that can lead us out of our lonely story and back into the great togetherness that I know we are all craving. And I share because this is what we humans have always done, in every culture. We have created beauty as a way back to remembering ourselves, as a way of getting through the hard times, as a way of taking care of each other and of speaking the language of soul, myth, Earth, and magic.

The One That Escaped

I did not begin making altars to share.

Actually, far from it. At first, they were very personal. Precious even. They let me step away from the incessantly oversharing, "look at me" culture that social media propagates and to be a kid again, playing carelessly without any need to impress anyone. It was just my imagination and the land, from start to finish. And during the months after my breakup, as the altars became a reliable way to console my broken heart, I had a steadfast rule *not* to share my creations. The healing they offered was for me and me alone, and I felt too vulnerable to put my work out onto a bigger stage for others to consume. I was determined to hold on tightly to my creations. And then one day, one escaped me.

It was the afternoon on a rainy February day, and I was distracting myself with some Facebook scrolling to avoid the work that had piled up on my desk. As I mindlessly flipped through my newsfeed, there it was! Right in front of my eyes, an altar I had made just a few days before, posted by a friend (who tagged me) of a friend, someone I had never met and didn't know. Under the photo of the altar a caption cried out: "I was having the absolute worst day ever. My landlord let me know that she was moving back into my home and I had 30 days to move out. And only an hour later, my car got broken into and all my stuff stolen. Time for a timeout from life. I needed to escape, and pronto, and so I went to the park to walk and figure this all out. Where was I going to live, why now and why me??! I was looking for signs as to what to do because I seriously didn't know. Toward the end of my walk, just when I had almost given up and decided to leave my life here in California, I came across this—this magical cre-

> You need witnesses for wonder. Some things in life are too hard to see by yourself because they take up the whole sky, or because they happen every day, unwinding above your busyness, or because you thought you knew them already.
>
> —Stephen Jenkinson

ation. I have no idea who made it, when or why but damn, did my faith get renewed in an instant. The sign I got was to trust in the mystery and not to be afraid. So to whomever made this, even if it was a bunch of little fairies who worked all night, thank you. You renewed me."

As you can imagine, I was floored. Something I made that I thought was invisible to everyone but me had been found by someone I didn't know, and it had helped them

through some really challenging circumstances. Beyond any intention of mine, they discovered it and it gave them a much-needed gift. And now, as she shared her story and a photograph of my little-altar-that-could, she was giving a gift back to me. I wondered what else was possible with these altars if I stopped keeping them all to myself and gave them their wings to fly, for clearly they wanted to.

To be honest, I tried many times to send them off. I photographed every altar I made that week and was ready to cast them out into the vast ocean of social media, like scrolls corked in glass bottles, when the entourage of my saboteur arrived in my head just in time to stop me. They came to burden me with judgment.

I was afraid how they would be received. It felt like some part of my heart was on display in this work, something so tender and unspoken that I was scared that if I let them out into the world, they would be laughed at, rejected, or worse, just considered insignificant. I wasn't making altars so that they would be liked. I was making them to renew my own humanity every day, to connect me back to the magic of the natural world and my own creative impulses. If I was going to share it to get liked, I decided I wouldn't share it at all; but if there was a deeper purpose, to let them serve in ways that I couldn't even imagine, like the one that got away, then I was willing to let them have a life of their own.

So I started with a small experiment.

I took a photograph of a very simple circular altar I made out of only eucalyptus buttons, all faded and worn from the dusty soil, and sent it by text message to a bunch of friends. I knew they all loved me, and I banked on them being receptive to whatever way I chose to express myself. I mean, isn't that what friends are for? So I attached a photo of the altar and wrote something like:

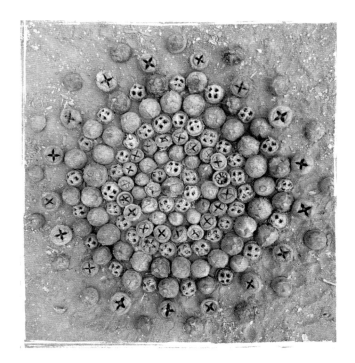

"A little gift for your day and a reminder to pay attention to and delight in the simple things."

There was no response for some time. *Ah, well, I thought, that was that. First and last one shared. Maybe those voices spoke some truth—that this was probably just an exercise meant for me, like some doodles in a notebook.* I wondered if perhaps the altar that had helped that stranger was an anomaly. The lack of response from my friends was clear evidence that they were just too busy, uninterested, or unaffected by my offering. *Glad I tested it out, I concluded. I'm never doing that again.*

But I had called the game too early. I apparently needed to give it some time. My friends began to text back. And what I received astonished me. It seemed that this little reminder to stay attuned to the simple wonders of their day was what each one of them needed. They weren't just placating me, there was authentic gratitude in their response. How did I know? Because my tiny gift to them inspired and spawned more gifts, either back to me or to others in their lives. This is what Lewis Hyde refers to when he says, "The gift grows as a result of its circulation."

One friend, who is a single mother, let me know that she was feeling terribly isolated that morning, so she took her kids outside and played in the earth with them. They collected and assembled art out of everything laying around in their backyard. Another friend, who was stuck inside her office cubicle, said she felt compelled to do something creative too. She texted me back a haiku, which she printed and hung next to her computer. Other friends sent quotes, photos, notes of gratitude, and other stories of ways they got inspired. This wasn't just an "oh, pretty" response. The inspiration was contagious. I passed my friends a little handmade beauty and it grew into more beauty.

They also pleaded for me to continue. And so I did. Every day, for many weeks, I chose a new friend to be the recipient of this altar gift. I texted them a little message of what I myself needed to hear that day along with a picture of the altar, saying that I hoped it would also serve their life as well.

I'll let you in on something: the sabotaging voice in my head, the voice so concerned with "me," has never truly gone away. Even after making thousands of altars over the years and touching tens of thousands of people's lives, I still am faced with the question: Does any of this matter?

As the world burns, immigrants face deportations, species go extinct, the threat of a world war looms, and people battle depression and mental illness, I'm left wondering how sharing a little bit of earth art helps any of this. Can it? Am I doing anything at all? And just when I'm about to give up for the thousandth time, I remember that this isn't really about me at all. That the true gift of art, as Hyde says, is to "draw each of its participants into a wider self." The altars, and art in general, have the ability to connect us back into a greater union, a larger body. Art shows us that we are more than just individuals who live our own separate lives. In a way, art calls us back home.

This remembering is even hidden in the word *art* itself. The word finds its origins from the Proto-Indo-European word *ar(ə)-ti,* which is a suffixed form of the root *ar,* meaning "to fit together." Like that which joins all the bones in a body, art's function is to bring the many separate pieces temporarily into one, which is where we get the Old French word *articulation,* meaning "joints." Art joins us. It articulates a bridge between the artist's imagination and the audience's imagination, between the creative spirit and the material world, between chaos and order, and between the seen and the unseen. Art remembers wholeness. It crosses boundaries, borders, and time to bring us back to our shared humanity, to our living world, to our family, community and ancestry, to the spiraling cycles of time and to the deeper meaning of what really matters and has always mattered. Art humbles us by weaving us back into our small, necessary place in the great enduring mystery of things.

To me, art and nature cultivate trust. Trust that we are not alone. Trust that what separates us can also bring us back together. And trust that even the smallest of things, these earth altars, can be a beauty bridge that welcomes us across the divide and back into the grace of connection. Beauty, the poet David Whyte says, is "an achieved state of both deep attention and self-forgetting; the self-

forgetting of seeing, hearing, smelling or touching that erases our separation, our distance, our fear of the other. Beauty invites us, through entrancement, to that fearful frontier between what we think makes us; and what we think makes the world."

When Whyte speaks to that fearful edge between remembering and forgetting, between us and the rest of the world, I think he is asking us to let go of ourselves more and to trust in that kind of surrender. The self-conscious mind is so concerned with how things look or sound, if it's good enough, or if it will be received well, that it prevents us from opening ourselves to the gift that wants to move through us.

I recently watched a video of Joyce DiDonato, a voice professor at Juilliard who was teaching a young tenor, Joshua Blue, not just to sing but to conjure something through his singing. He was clearly a bit shy, but he was really trying, and maybe that was the issue. She kept on pulling him by the hand around the stage, courting him to sense the romance longing to be expressed in the Italian lyrics of Donizetti's *L'elisir d'amore* and to give his voice over as a bridge to the other world. She was pleading with him to let go of himself so that a connection could occur—so that the beauty could enter through him and so the audience could be taken by it too.

My gift is to communicate my heart in this universal language of symmetry and nature, what some people call mandalas. Perhaps the gift can awaken a moment, both in myself and in you, of connection—to a timeless, enchanted universe where balance and beauty can help us let go of ourselves and call us back toward the whole, both to the Earth and to the collective imagination that we share. Doing this requires my willingness to make the art and then to let it exist beyond me and my self-

conscious, reflective, concerned, hopeful, and fearful mind; to let it live into the world and meet you there. And vice versa. That is how we maintain these beautiful gifts and keep them alive. As I once heard Stephen Jenkinson say, "The only way to truly care for something is to put it out into the river of life."

What I've come to discover by sharing my art and letting it find its own way in the world is that, thankfully, I'm not the only one who knows how to speak this language. Many of us are remembering how beauty and nature are languages that can bring us together. Share your earth arrangements across the vast oceans and valleys, across the boundaries that separate us, and let your blazing brilliant imagination awaken us to each other, as life calls to life.

THE PHOTOGRAPH: AN EXERCISE

I don't always take photographs of my work. Sometimes my earth altar is only a whispered love letter that exists undocumented between myself and the land.

But for the most part, I do photograph these creations as a memory that evokes that day's encounter and my conversation with the natural world. Because none of my art lasts—the leaves crumble, the plums shrivel, and the flowers wither—the photograph remembers the life cycle of the art. I photograph my work at its inception, at the height of its life and during its decay. I want to document the work as a whole life, with a beginning, middle, and ending, watching it return back to where it came.

When I photograph my art at its most symmetrical, there is an inherent tension, for that is when the work balances on the edge between creation and destruction. At that moment, I want the photograph to capture the altar teetering back and forth between my influence and the influence of nature. I want change to be felt in the photograph, so that you can almost feel the wind that's about to come and blow it all away.

The grandfather of modern ephemeral art and one of my great influences, Andy Goldsworthy, says this about his photography: "Each work grows, stays, decays—integral parts of a cycle which the photograph shows at its height, marking the moment when the work is most alive. There is an intensity about a work at its peak that I hope is expressed in the image. Process and decay are implicit in that moment."

So here's my assignment to you:

Take three photographs:

- One of your altar's birth. This can be during your wander, after you sweep, or during the very first shape you place down on the ground.
- One at the height of your altar's life. This is when you finish building and step away for the first time.
- One of its decay. This can be minutes or days later.

Let the photography capture your entire process and don't just focus on the end goal. Impermanent art is never static and is always changing, so see if you can let your photograph tell that story.

Don't let the photography interrupt your focus or presence with the art as you document the different stages of its life. The phone or camera should be a tool to help you share the beauty and not distract you from it. So only take your phone or camera out during these three stages of this assignment.

Chapter 7

LET GO

**Is not impermanence
the very fragrance of our days?**

—*Rainer Maria Rilke*

Not Made to Last

The berries roll, the leaves shift, the flowers wilt ... and what you made no longer looks like what you intended it to. You must confront the inevitable—that the beauty you made isn't meant to last. There are other forces here that want to play too, reminding you of the only constant in life: Change.

Impermanence is like the guest you never wanted. He enters without knocking, tosses all of your neatly placed things around, eats everything in your cupboard, and leaves your home in shambles. No matter how much you try, this guest will somehow find his way inside and will have his way with all the things of your life. This is just how it is.

But what if you didn't resist this guest? What if you not only invited impermanence in but even offered him the best seat in your home, the best food on your table, and treated him as the honorable guest you've been expecting? What if you treated him as a teacher who came to remind you that impermanence underwrites the very nature of your life and life itself?

Our earth altar is ultimately a gift to this venerable, wild guest. He will toss it, eat it, and blow it apart, and all of that is proper, for this beauty was made to change. Actually, our practice here is an exercise in letting go of our own need to always be in control and in charge, for that is what change truly asks of us.

This last, seventh, movement is about letting go. It says, enough is enough; put it down and leave it be—you did your best to organize and order your altar. You arranged everything as you wanted it, and now let change have its way with it. Yielding control is how we can allow ourselves to come to understand and love the fullness of things, even and especially their endings.

And that's the real treasure that this guest is entrusting to us. If we let him, impermanence arrives to teach us to deliciously, unabashedly, brokenheartedly fall in love with what is here right now because that's all we have. As you watch your altar return to the disorder it came from, as the leaves crumble, the berries shrivel, and the feathers blow away, let your heart open wide enough and your presence be full enough to let it be.

Blown away. Devoured. Destroyed.
Torn apart. Decomposing. Returning.
In seconds and days,
your creation changes.

Release

I recently watched another episode of one of my favorite Netflix series, *Chef's Table*. I noticed a tool that almost all of these world-famous chefs have clipped to their shirts: a tweezer. This tool is made for those truly delicate moments, when the single strand of seaweed has to be positioned in the perfect place as it hangs off the mountain of miso or when that one lavender blossom must be arranged in such a way that it seems like the entire dish is dependent on it being exactly next door to the coriander seed. These tweezers let the chef become a human magnifying glass, so that the entrée no longer becomes just food but more like an artistic masterpiece. And as I watch their laser-beam concentration, a dedication to arranging the dish exactly the way they want it to look, I find myself relating with every bone in my body.

But here's the thing. There comes a point when all the labors of that dish, the cooking, preparing, plating, and placing must leave the chef's eagle eye and get carried out to the customer's table to be eaten. No matter how intricately these chefs fixate on the dish, no matter how attentively they work those tweezers to make it look exactly as they see it, the food eventually gets taken away from them. And that's the whole point. While we marvel at the chef's efforts, these dishes are made to be eaten. The chef must eventually put those tweezers down in order for the dish to be served up and enjoyed by those eating at the restaurant.

There is always a moment while creating when we have to open our hands and let go of the thing we care about most. But how do we know when it's time to do that? How do we know when to let go?

> Everything is in process. Everything— every tree, every blade of grass, all the animals, insects, human beings, buildings, the animate and the inanimate— is always changing, moment to moment.
>
> —*Pema Chödrön*

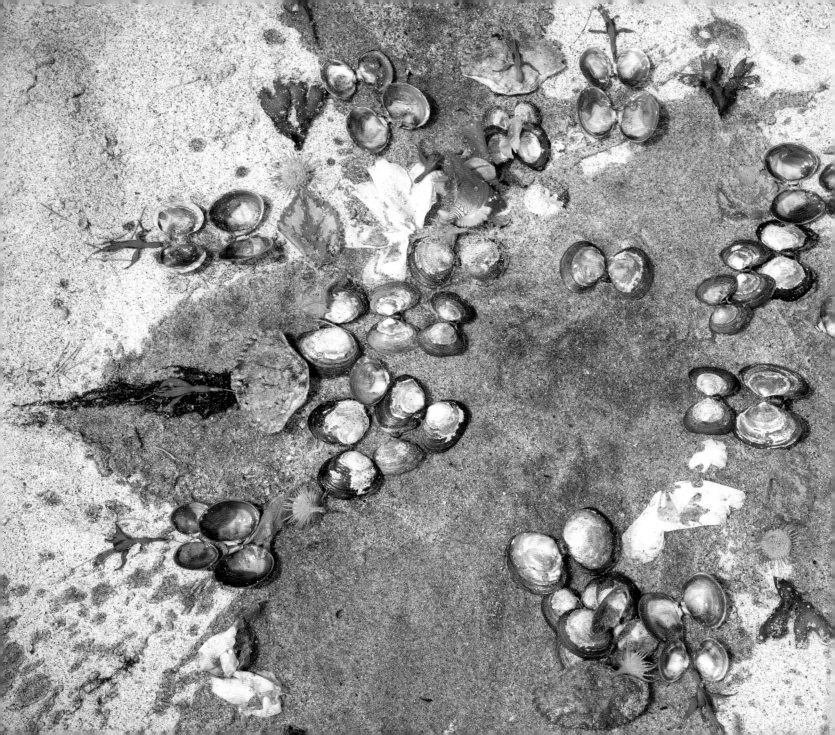

There are two voices to listen to when letting go—your own readiness (and choosing) and a larger outside force that asks, or rather demands, that you do so. I have chosen to let go of many altars because I could recognize the completion of my vision and the art was done. And yet, at other times, my hands were forced to let go because the sun was setting, the flowers died, or the whole thing got blown away. Learning how to listen to these voices can deeply inform other moments of your life when you choose, or are forced, to let go of something you love.

I've always been attracted to this process of creating and letting go. The first time I saw Andy Goldsworthy's documentary *Rivers and Tides* I watched one particular scene over and over again because his process captivated and inspired me. He would rise at dawn and find his way to the edge of a bay before the tide came in, and there he spent the whole morning building a nestlike shape out of driftwood that stood almost 15 feet in diameter. He labored in the early morning frost up until the very last moment, when the tide would come in and literally pick up this nest and dramatically carry it away into the water. He would build his art on the edge of where water met earth or where stone met sky, places where he eventually had to release his work because those edges were dynamic and changing. All he could do was watch his art dissolve in the water or evaporate in the air or fall to the earth. Sometimes this seemed to frustrate him because the release happened before he wanted it to, and other times the moment of destruction miraculously came at the perfect moment, like when that nest silently drifted off into the bay.

Recently, I made the outrageous decision to try and make a Morning Altar out of mourning dove feathers on a hill during a windstorm. In all fairness, the wind didn't pick up until I was in the middle of building. But my instinctual response to the wind was absolute resistance. My whole body tensed and the voice in my head screamed Go away! I tried to finish arranging the feathers, but as I put one down another one would pop up.

My eyes strained, my hands grasped, and my belly knotted itself into a tight ball as I forced the altar into the look I wanted. I was reluctant to give up, but then I recognized that letting go isn't actually giving up. The difference is in the approach. Giving up is a kind of passive collapse, whereas letting go is opening around change because change has something to offer. I chose to stop resisting. I knew that elemental force was greater than my determination to control the pieces of the altar,

and as I released those feathers back into the wind, my body echoed that movement—my eyes went from strained to soft, my jaw went from clenched to relaxed, my hands went from grasped to open, and my stomach went from tight to loose. My body eased as I surrendered the art back out into the world, and I received the joy of letting it all go.

Buddhism teaches there is nothing in life that is solid, graspable, or reliable. Sometimes it may feel like the ground has dropped away from under us. The Buddhist monk Pema Chödrön calls this "groundlessness." She teaches that inner strength, flexibility, and openness of mind and heart come from our capacity to be more comfortable with the fact that things are always shifting and changing. "That is the nature of reality and rather than that being bad news and unsettling, it actually frees us up to see each moment as unique and fresh and each personal encounter as happening for the first time."

Letting go takes daily practice, and this is the skill we are exercising when making a Morning Altar. By spending some time once a day making something precise and beautiful and then letting it go, we strengthen our capacity not to just allow change but also to build a relationship with change as the fundamental constant in life.

I've even found that this concept and practice is at play during my morning yoga practice. After an hour of intense stretching and focus, which builds up the energy and heat, yoga concludes with the last posture called *savasana* or "corpse pose." This posture is, as my friend, yoga teacher, and author Marisa Weppner wrote to me, "the highest act of surrender, when we allow the muscles that were just a moment ago working so hard, and the resolute focus of the mind that was trained on breath and body awareness, to ebb back into the Self." My whole body gets to release its efforts and surrender it all to "the sweetness of that one precious moment."

I recently had a conversation with a friend who toured all over the country with Tibetan monks for four years making sand mandalas. His story captivated me as he described the exactness of their process. They would draw out a chalk-lined grid on the table where the mandala would be created, measuring exact mathematical dimensions for the design. The monks would have certain tools handy, called chak-pur, that would help them lay down the sand in very controlled ways. And it wasn't just the measurements or control of hand that impressed me, but also their impeccably placed prayers.

Every color, every squiggle, every scoop of sand all had a particular prayer assigned to it. For instance, if a mandala had a deer in it, they wouldn't see it just as an image of a deer. They saw it as an entity that they wanted to bring forth with these prayers so that this deer-spirit would be willing to be housed in the mandala. These monks had studied and memorized thousands of prayers that they would utter while building the mandala, imbuing the sand and process with their holy words and energy. At completion, the whole colorful, geometric mandala became a holy sandcastle housing the prayers, animals, and entities in a gorgeous yet impermanent structure. And as you probably know, the ultimate practice for the Tibetan sand mandalas is its deconstruction after its completion. These remarkably impeccable creations, which sometimes take weeks to make, are brushed into the center, creating what my friend called a "pile of prayers." The sand is then released into a nearby flowing body of water, where the currents carry it all over the world, thereby spreading the prayers and their healing.

Taking the sand and letting the water carry it away is a great example of how the monks practice being in a relationship of pure control and then surrender. They build an impeccable work of art and then let all of their prayers and efforts return to a source greater than them. In this way they can remember that the only thing that is permanent is impermanence.

My own Jewish tradition had this process as well. A biblical practice called Shmita, otherwise known as the Year of Release, recognized the collective need not to just build, accomplish, and create but also to release, rest, and return as a way to keep the culture healthy. Traditionally, every seventh year on the calendar cycle would be a sabbatical year, similar to the concept of the seventh day of the week, Sabbath, where instead of individuals resting, the entire culture practiced letting go.

In a way, the Year of Release is a like a big exhale for the entire culture. In that exhale, my ancestors got to remember their relationship with the wild and the great mysterious world that they existed within. They let go to be replenished.

What I've come to understand is how the practice of releasing and letting go is just as important as the practice of building and growing.

In the same way the exhale is just as necessary as the inhale; or the dark quiet of winter is just as needed as the bright activity of summer, we must discover practices that help us let go so that we can have a direct relationship with impermanence, mystery, and groundlessness.

For that is the true nature of life—it is always changing and moving, and it is never static. And the true art of living is to get good at being curious, limber, fearless, and even joyful in the presence of change, in the presence of life.

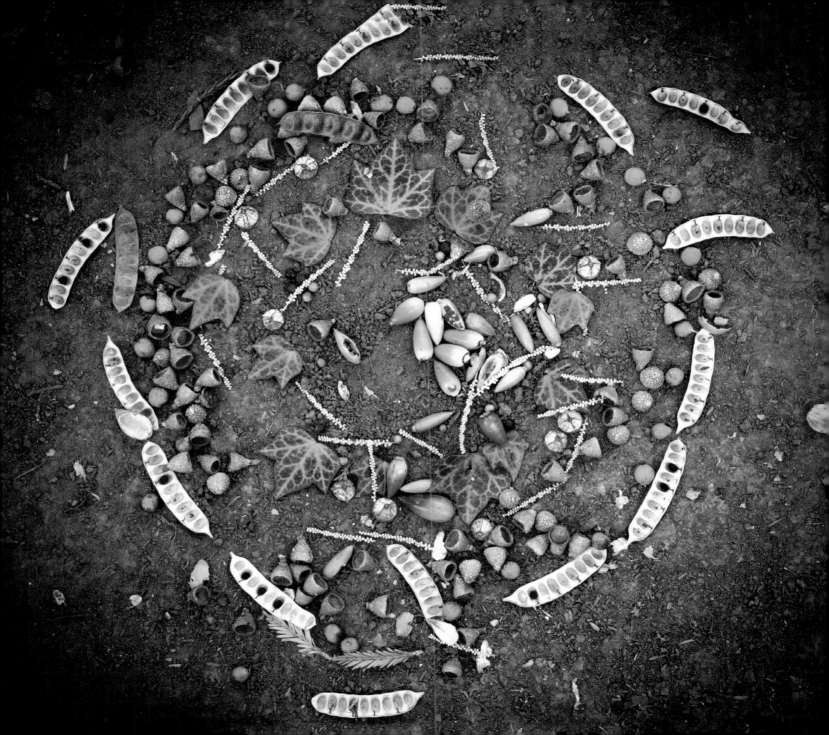

The Puff That Got Away

About two years ago, I was out hiking the hills with one of my best friends. It was an especially windy day in the Bay Area. This friend is the kind of person who can turn an everyday hike into an epic adventure.

Although we were completely taken by the worlds we were conjuring for each other, I somehow noticed that off to the west, near a ridge that dropped down into the eucalyptus forest whose branches were blowing around quite a bit that day, there was something growing that I had never seen before! Sprouting about four feet from the ground, there was an enormous patch of, I don't know what else to call them, puff globes. They were about the size of a small melon, and they seemed almost prehistoric. Looking both so fragile and dominant, these puffs were comprised of the littlest seed-umbrellas that sprouted from the center that, when combined together, created an orblike effect. It was like those little dandelion puffs you may have blown and wished upon as a kid, but this puff globe was ten times bigger.

As an earth artist, finding a plant like this is akin to a choreographer meeting his dance muse who would inspire his next composition of ballets. While fawning over this plant, I received a vision of an altar that I had to make with a puff globe as the centerpiece. And, since you've read the earlier chapters of this book and know that I don't just harvest plants without permission, I got down on my hands and knees and serenaded this plant with a love song like I never had before and promised to create a majestic altar that would be worthy of such beauty. I could sense the permission I needed to harvest her, and so I did. I started carrying what looked like a magical wand, with a glowing orb on its top, on a day

when the wind made herself quite pronounced. Playtime with my friend was over; it was time to boogie and get home.

I cradled that plant like I would my own baby, doing my best to try and keep it protected from anything that would harm it. We walked fast and it seemed like The Graces were being kind to me that day. Treasure in hand, with only about 30 more steps to go, my thoughts turned to planning my next task, which was to find a way to store this harvest in my home until the next day when, at dawn, I would begin to make some art with it. But then, just when I stepped onto my driveway, literally the moment I put my foot on that stone, a wind came, like the flash of a whip, and blew this orb to smithereens. I looked up and saw all those mini umbrellas being carried off; I looked down and the only thing left in my hand was the shaft of the wand, the magic gone.

I felt my friend's hand on my shoulder. She understood. My head dropped, as did hers, and we stood there in silence, saddened by what was lost and acknowledging the powerful reminder that we don't always get what we want. There are forces so much larger than us at play, forces that change the course of things and your life is subject to its power, blowing you off your best set plans and casting you out once again with empty hands that once were full. As an earth artist, I am in collaboration and cahoots with the natural world, a world that is always changing, never predictable, and quite humbling. The sensation that visits me when practicing my art outside, is smallness. That is, how small I feel in the midst of it all, reminding me that in geological time my life too is just an impermanent seed here temporarily, until it is gone.

Even though that wand with the glowing orb was no longer, I still carried the vision of what I wanted to see created. So I hatched a plan. I had less than a week until I left for the summer, and I knew that these plants would not be seeding in the same way when I returned, and so I committed myself, twice a day, to return to the same spot on the hill overlooking the eucalyptus forest, just in case any more puffs flowered. Every dawn and every dusk, I climbed to the top of the hill to scout for sprouts and, while I consistently came home empty handed, I didn't lose my faith.

And wouldn't you know it, on the day of my departure, my stubbornness paid off.

The wind was alive and well that day, and so I carried a shoebox, just in case. And there, in the rising light, still faintly golden as it peaked above the hills, were not one but two puffs that had flowered overnight. I sat down at the base of the plants, fed its thirsty roots with water I had brought, put a pinch of tobacco in the palm of my hands, and made my plea, "I don't know why I'm so drawn to you, plant, and the ways you come alive, like magic growing from the earth. I don't know if it's my place to ask again, this time I'm requesting both of your flowers, but I'm willing to be bold and do so. Would you be willing to let me harvest again?"

At first I didn't get an answer. I sat there in silence and waited. And, as you can probably guess, I received the go-ahead to harvest both puffs.

I hurried home with my gift in hand. I went down to Wildcat Creek and faithfully practiced the movements of a Morning Altar, sitting with the place and sweeping the earth to create an empty circle ready to receive my vision. That morning I had also harvested some equisetum, an ancient plant that some consider it to be a living fossil because for over 100 million years it dominated the understory of the late Paleozoic Era forests. Because of the wind, I decided to build the entire altar first and to let the orbs be the last crowning moment.

I built the structure of the piece, arranging the equisetum so that it looked like the vision in my mind. When I looked at the time, it seemed like I had just the right amount of leeway to finish the altar, photograph it, and get myself to the airport. And so I opened the shoebox and took out one of the two orbs and placed it in the center of the altar, feeling so satisfied that my vision had become real when *bam*, a gust of wind came and kicked the orb from the altar, rolling it off the edge and into the creek. "*No!*" I cried. I couldn't believe how close I was to finishing and how uncertain this entire enterprise seemed.

I then spoke directly to the wind: "Dear spirit of the wind," I prayed, "You are probably laughing with how much effort I've put into making something so fragile, that you can so easily undo—as you have shown me twice this week—and yet, I am so close to producing the vision I've longed to bring forward. Please, please spirit of the wind, if you could hear my plea and ease your gusts for just a few minutes, I will be forever grateful."

Silence. This was my window. I hesitantly cracked open the shoebox, understanding the value of what was inside, and let my hand reach in and cup the second orb ever

so slightly like it was the living offspring of earth and air, and I placed it gently on the center of the altar. I was shaking from trying to keep my cool, though I knew what I wanted to do, which was to photograph the culmination of my vision before its inevitable fate. But, as I went to get the shot, the wind jokingly nudged the orb a little so that it rolled off the altar, but not down the creek. The orb was still intact—*phew*—but I was reminded again as to how temporary this whole arrangement was. So I gen-

tly retrieved the orb, put it back as the centerpiece, and snapped five photographs. The moment lasted all of 15 seconds, and then the wind decided it had had enough and blew it apart, releasing those little seed-umbrellas from their tension of togetherness.

It happened. I sat down to collect myself and let out a little hallelujah for the small but meaningful achievement. Although this photograph can never tell the story of what actually happened, it is merely a frozen record of

a windless moment of perfection. I knew the real story. And now, so do you.

It was an experience that made me feel, in every cell of my body, the tension between what I wanted and the inevitable force of change.

Creating art that doesn't last lets me understand the world I inhabit and the language this world speaks. My art exists in nature and allows me to practice speaking in the language nature speaks. Our Earth is always changing, growing and dying, over and over again. The more you spend time with her, the more she is asking you to learn the lesson that you, too, and all you hold dear, are part of this reality. And by learning to speak this language well, you also learn the real language of gratitude.

Sometimes with my art, change is fun, exciting, and satisfying. This is manifestly true when it works out, as in the story I just told. And yet, more often than not, it doesn't work in my favor. In those moments, I am faced with my resistance to change, to all the ways I demand things be how I want them to be. I get to see myself as a little boy crying so that he can get his way. The Earth tutors me to exercise a greater capacity, which is to learn that change is not something to prevent but is a way of life, of being a human being.

In a culture that is so obsessed with being young and living forever, a culture that is so undeniably at war with change and impermanence, so fearful of uncertainty, this art's power and wisdom lies in its temporariness. Because it plays with the tension of change and lives on the ephemeral edge, it remembers an older and deeper wisdom that we often resist at the personal and cultural level: to practice unattachment and become more comfortable with the ever-changing nature of reality.

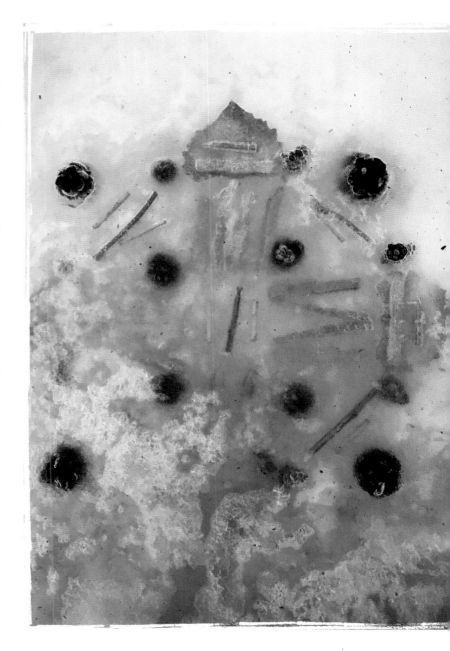

Loss into Beauty

This past spring, my little wandering companion left this world. Rudy, a stout and stubborn miniature schnauzer, was buried under the two towering redwood trees down by the creek. The morning after her death, about seven of my friends and I dug a hole and filled it with wild chamomile flowers, fennel branches, desert sage stems, shells from our favorite beach, and the salty drips and drops from all of our tears as we buried her little body in the ground. That entire morning we sang sad songs underneath those redwood trees as they cried too, with the rain from the previous night's storm still dripping from their branches. A lot of tears were spilt that morning as we all came to terms with the loss of our "little bear."

Looking down on this freshly covered grave of bare earth, I felt compelled to lay down an altar. I arranged a circle of pinecones around the hole she was buried in and let my tears mingle with the altar I was creating. Raven feathers and bay leaves filled the space and made the grave look like a circling wheel, as I imagined my best friend traveling back over the stars to her ancestral dog pack. I spent a couple of hours arranging this altar while letting my grief make something beautiful for her and for all of us. This is a way I've come to know how to express love.

I have often heard my teacher ask the question, "What does it take to fall in love with being alive?" It makes you consider your default knee-jerk response; when you are healthy, happy, busy, and all the pieces seem to be falling into place properly; when you have what you want and it seems like it will be this way for a long, long time. It's easy to love life then, but this is only loving the part of life you prefer, the life you approve of and that works for you and everyone around you.

I can hear my teacher pleading for me to dig even deeper. That perhaps the understanding of love, and all of which you hold dear, is found by glimpsing its endings. That maybe loving life, truly and irrevocably, comes when you recognize that everything in your midst isn't going to last, yourself included, and then loving it all even more so. That kind of love asks us to let go of an imaginary future, where everything lives indefinitely, for the sake of really letting ourselves be in the midst of what is present in the here and now, albeit temporarily.

The many months before Rudy died really taught me about love. I was witnessing her in the last chapter of her life. While it was challenging and sad, it was also an experience that helped me locate my deep love for this dog and her life, because I knew she wasn't going to last. She was 16 and every day was another opportunity to witness time having its way with her. She taught me, through experiencing her ending, that my grief was actually a new way of loving her. I wasn't just loving the parts of her life that were familiar or easy, but I was learning to love all of her life, including her ending. It was through my heartbreak that I could feel a way of loving her, a way of loving that I hadn't felt before, a way that included my longing for her. "Grief is a way of loving," says Stephen Jenkinson, "and love is a way of grieving. They need each other in order to be themselves." My grief for Rudy was and is joined at the hip of my love for her.

Loss is an inevitable reality of life, for all that we hold dear will eventually leave us or we will eventually leave them. Yet, in this industrialized culture, we humans shun our eyes to this fundamental truth of life. Loss is consid-

ered an unwanted sign of failure, where something went wrong. This dominant culture, built on progress and growth, doesn't see loss as having a purpose other than something to overcome. There is so much effort made to avoid loss, such a struggle to keep it at bay for as long as we can. And even when loss becomes unavoidable, the cultural response is to "get through it" or "get over it" in order to get back to business as usual.

Many other cultures in the world teach their people how to grieve well, and do so communally. The Mohawk tribe's "condolence ritual" and the Jewish people's seven days of shiva provide just two examples. By contrast, our modern culture asks its people to suffer their grief privately. And even when someone dies in our lives, most people only get a week of bereavement from work to be with their loss, because the motivation and expectation is that they get back to living their normal lives again— not to let the grief interrupt too much. And yet that is

the whole point of grief. Grief is meant to interrupt our lives so that everyone can once again remember what is important and what matters.

What if we treated our grief not as an affliction but as a way to get to know life well? What if grief could be our own way of praising not just what we lost but also what we still have? What if grief was not something to try and get through but instead was a skill to get good at? What if grief was, as Toko-pa Turner says in her book, *Belonging*, "the downpour your soul has been thirsting for"? Grief is a visitor that comes to us with purpose. It arrives to tenderize our hearts. Grief helps us remem-

When you live this balanced way, with the endings sitting next to you as your beloved companion, and not banished because they are too sad or painful, you can practice loving all of life—its beginnings, middles, and endings for this is the natural order of things. Knowing love and loss in this way shapes you into a real human being. The poet Kahlil Gibran said, "The deeper that sorrow carves into your being, the more joy you can contain." What that means is that your love and joy for life is directly related to your capacity to know the bittersweet reality of loss. Love and loss are inexorably tied together, and they inform the other. Your willingness to know this, and not close your heart because of the way life is but to open it even wider knowing that grief and love, loss and life are two wings of the same bird, is the practice of becoming a compassionate, alive, and grateful human being.

Even though you may want so much of your life to last forever, grief tells us that it can't and shouldn't. And from that place, the heartbreak of knowing that life truly is impermanent and fleeting, is how we can, as Martín Prechtel says, "let grief turn our losses into beauty." For this is where our love for life flowers.

Because Rudy is buried on my land, I am able to visit her grave and altar almost every day. And every day I feel her loss. Over time I have let the hole in my life that Rudy left be filled with beauty for the whole world to have. Many altars have been made from this loss, and even this very book has been written from a brokenhearted place. I long for my sweet pup to be lying next to me as I write. But it is through that brokenness, through the tender, cracked, and open heart that came from Rudy's loss, that I understand what Leonard Cohen means when he says, "That's how the light gets in."

ber that all we have is only here temporarily and to find gratitude for that.

Renowned grief-practitioner and psychotherapist Francis Weller says, "The work of the mature person is to carry grief in one hand and gratitude in the other and to be stretched large by them. How much sorrow can I hold? That's how much gratitude I can give. If I carry only grief, I'll bend toward cynicism and despair. If I have only gratitude, I'll become saccharine and won't develop much compassion for other people's suffering. Grief keeps the heart fluid and soft, which helps make compassion possible."

Through the Looking Box

I like to revisit my altars, like old friends, days after making them. Because they are made of living things and are made in a living place, they always change dramatically from what they once were. The term *ephemeral* literally means "for only a day." And as an altar decays, sinks, unravels, or gets blown away over days, it tells another story—of weather, of temperature, of animal visitation, and of transformation. The natural world takes the art from my hands to hers.

Recently, I made an altar on the most unlikely of places—on the face of a frozen creek. That particular bend in the creek doesn't see any sun in the winter, and so the ice just builds and builds on top of itself creating an array of featherlike crystals on its surface. The ice and water is always changing into each other, and so I wanted to experiment building a piece on something more active and unpredictable than the ground.

I spent a day gathering river rocks and cottonwood leaves and bits of this and that, which had fallen around the creek's shore. As I knelt down beside the inlet where I would build, I realized that only the surface had frozen. Water was flowing generously underneath. Interesting! I wondered how much weight that thin layer of ice would hold if I were to put stones and slate, bark, and branches on it. I would soon find out.

As I built up the altar, it seemed the ice held fast to the

rocks. Actually, too fast. Holding the rocks in my hand heated them up just enough that as I put them down on the ice, they got locked into place. When making art, I usually have the leeway to pick up and move pieces around at my discretion, but not so with this cold canvas. It took to everything quite quickly, even at times the skin on my hands. I discovered that I had to be quite deliberate with my placement before the ice froze the stones or me.

That evening the temperatures dropped into the single digits. The next morning I went back to the creek to visit my friend and see what had changed or if it even still was there. To my surprise, those feathery crystals had begun to grow onto the rock overnight, not just securing them but almost climbing onto them, claiming them.

Throughout that week, I returned every day and every time I documented the altar. Each day it got one step closer to being devoured and consumed by the ice. Over time, a frozen window-like pane formed on the surface of the art, such that you could still see the altar but only through that pane of ice. I once heard a story from an older woman who, as a child, would make "looking boxes" by digging a hole in the earth, creating what she called a fairy village out of leaves and berries inside the hole, and then putting a pane of glass over it. She said the glass made it feel like she was gazing into another world, especially as the moisture clouded the windowpane. This ice window over my altar felt just like that.

The altar was frozen in time, and after a while I stopped visiting it. But one day, weeks later, the temperatures rose dramatically. On an early January day, the sun made the ice melt and it feel like the desert again. My curiosity got me wondering what happened to the art. I walked down to the bend in the creek, which the sun still never reached, and as I approached I noticed that much of the creek was flowing with water again, especially around the place that housed the altar. As I peered into the water, I saw it! The ice had melted away so quickly that the stones and slate had sunk to the bottom of the creek. While the leaves had washed away, the river rocks had, in a strange and magical way, kept a similar symmetry and arrangement but now were completely under water. Instead of looking through the solid window of ice, I was now peering through the current of the stream and into another world.

While all of my altars have an ending, it would be more accurate to call this a transformation. The pieces I collect continue their journey onward and only temporarily sit in an ordered arrangement on the altar. Some of them decompose and become earth again, others are eaten, while some pieces, like those rocks, remain nested in a new home on the creek's bed. At times, this all seems like a greater commentary on life and feels quite poetic. Jane Hirshfield says that "Poetry's work is not simply the recording of inner or outer perception; it makes by words and music new possibilities of perceiving." I find this is true for me as well. Making earth art opens me up to the playing in a much bigger world where humans are not at the center. Rather, I am in a playground or an artist studio with many greater-than-human collaborators, all influencing and changing the art. As Hirshfield goes on to say, "A work of art is not a piece of fruit lifted from a tree branch: it is a ripening collaboration of artist, receiver, and world." Witnessing an altar's ephemerality over time offers me a wondrous looking box into the true nature of this world, which is always and forever changing.

THE BASICS:
Letting Go

Eventually, you must walk away
from your altar.
Let the material you collected
return to the earth.
Remember that impermanence is life.
Nothing lasts forever.
Especially your Morning Altar.
And that's at the heart of this practice.
Come back later that day or every few days
and witness what happens.
Witness change.
And begin again.

CONCLUSION

But wherever we
are right now,
whatever our lives are
like in the moment,
this is our mandala,
our working basis
for awakening.

—*Pema Chödrön*

A Detective of Delight

My five-year-old self never once questioned the purpose of making beautiful art from nature. My whole being always came alive while doing it. Exploring the backyard let me wander into another world that welcomed my imagination as the alchemical ingredient that brought this world to life. Broken sticks made stars on the earth, and fallen leaves arranged just so could conjure the face of a deep-sea creature or a rarely seen tree spirit. This little boy dreamed with his hands. He concocted creations for hours and hours, and the backyard became a constellation of universes and myths that swirled infinitely around his imagination. As a co-creator with the Earth, I became an explorer of wonder, an astronaut of curiosity, and a detective of delight. I understood myself more when I was seeing who I was in the reflection and enchantment of the Earth. Playing with rocks and moss, making shapes with flowers and grass stalks, and decorating those little wormholes provided me with an endless treasure trove of resources to help flesh out my imaginative, creative self and to recognize my kinship with nature.

Thirty years later, during the most devastating breakup of my life, the Earth offered herself once again as a resource to process and metabolize my grief. Those early mornings spent wandering around the foggy hills of Wildcat Canyon with my dog while foraging for neighborhood treasure reminded me that even though I was in pain, there was not only immense beauty in the world but that I could understand my own pain by making beauty from it. Sitting under that eucalyptus tree on a hilltop overlooking the Bay at dawn each morning let me find my way back to myself as my imagination met the Earth. Time and time again, this practice calmed my mind and

faithfully brought me back to life by plugging me into the magical realms of curiosity and creativity. My hands started dreaming again. Eventually, because I loved it so much, it became a daily creative ritual and resource that continues to keep me grounded and connected. Even yesterday, after creating another altar on the frozen creek here in Boulder Mountain, Utah, I surprised myself by wondering how it could be that something so small and simple, something so utterly impermanent—and arranged from the stuff most people step on—could make me feel so alive, so purposeful and connected to all of life.

This connection ripples out well beyond me. I once created an altar in an alleyway in the Mission District of San Francisco where I lived. The alley was dirty, a gritty place of graffiti and cracked concrete, but I was inspired to make something beautiful in the city. So I set myself down and created a circular altar made with magnolia leaves and ripe orange dates bursting out into sunrays. As I worked on it all day, I noticed an inspired little girl who had taken some of the material I had gathered and created a much smaller mandala near mine, almost like a small planet in orbit around my sun. And then, to my surprise, her mother joined in to create her own next to her daughter's, which attracted another mother and her small child. Within an hour, that alley had spontaneously filled with over a dozen people of all ages, ethnicities, and economic realities creating an entire galaxy of circular planets, moons, suns, and stars made from leaves and branches offered by the city's street trees. People who usually would ignore each other on the sidewalk were on their hands and knees making beauty side by side, inspired by a little girl's desire to play along. This was the power of earth art in action, the power of bringing differences into one togetherness.

In a time that is so fractured and disempowered, at a time when so many people are longing for meaning and fulfillment, when the speed of our days seem to move faster than we can handle, when the need to be productive and capable eclipse our ability to be playful, healthy, and curious, and when feelings of hopelessness, isolation, and division shut us off from connecting to one another and our greater-than-human world, perhaps what is needed is a way back together again, both within ourselves and our larger community. Coming together means discovering soulful responses—what historian Thomas Berry calls, "moments of grace"—within our day and within our lives that transition us from a disruptive, distracted, and disconnected force to a mutually enhancing, creative, and life-giving presence on Earth. We must find our place again, both personally and collectively, not in dominance of but in relationship with our living planet. We must learn how to wonder again, how to slow down with the pace of our Earth and exercise our gorgeous imaginations every day, for these are some of the skills required of us so that we may respond to some of our greatest challenges ahead. As adults, we must remember these skills our children already instinctively have.

Morning Altars started out as my own way of responding to the challenges of my life. Being outside and making shapes with the Earth calmed my mind and opened my heart. But the more I made, the more I realized that this form of expression is so much greater than me. I see myself as part of an enormous lineage of earth artists, found in indigenous cultures from Peru and Thailand to Australia and here in America, who for thousands of years have understood the value and importance of making impermanent beauty with the land as a way of keeping their cultures healthy. With traditions like

India's rangolis, the Native American medicine wheels, or the Tibetan sand mandalas we witness how enduring and widespread this practice is. Through them we can come to realize that earth art is not only something beautiful but also is something that serves life. These peoples created earth altars as a way to heal illnesses, celebrate festivals, mark time, focus the mind, attract positive spirits and repel negative ones, grieve the dead, welcome the new babies, and feed the sacredness of the land. This ancient creative technology is a way that so many cultures around the world remember their kinship with their ancestors and the Earth, and they nourish that relationship with beauty so that it may continue to stay alive and well. It would serve us to look toward them as models for our own lives in these uncertain times.

Throughout the years, I have received a lot of mail from folks all over the world who have asked about my process. "Where do you get your material?" "Is there a bigger purpose for making them?" "Do you always photograph your art?" "Is the altar just left to decompose?" All these inquires inspired me to look at and reflect upon my own organic process, and that is how these seven movements were born. But there's a curious thing about these movements: The more I mindfully practice them, the more I discover how the very skills they strengthen are actually absent and forgotten from so many people's modern lives. For instance, most of us don't wander at all during our days, and instead we go from one planned thing or place to the next. But what are the consequences of a life free of wandering? More to the point, what crucial life skills do we lose when we always travel to where we think we should go? The more I teach the seven movements to make a Morning Altar, the more I have come to realize that each step of the practice addresses and strengthens a crucial human skill in which this culture and its people are deficient. At a certain point, I realized this wasn't just a ritual to make something beautiful. It is a ritual to get good at living beautifully.

This book's aim is to bring that beauty to a world that desperately needs it. However you engage with this book, whether you just view the images and let them enchant and delight you so that they might bring a brief moment of peace to your hectic day, or if you read it as an inspiration to get you outside and initiate your own Morning Altars practice because you can sense how your life and the lives around you would benefit from it, my hope is that this book brings you closer to the wonder of being alive on our incredible home planet floating in space.

It seems these days that real wonder, our capacity to be in the presence and awe of the mysteries of our existence on Earth, is in a state of atrophy and even decline. While we have more tech, information, and answers available to us than ever before, it has made us forget that wonder is a real skill that needs to be employed daily in order to befriend the unknown and make it miraculous. Wonder is the child of prayer and play. Rather than fear what we don't know, wonder lets us, as poet John O'Donohue says, "transfigure the anonymous into the intimate." It brings us back in touch with the simple, dynamic, unexplainable, and fantastic world, a world of infinite possibilities and awe that this book is devoted to.

I also hope that your journey through these pages reminds you of the preciousness of life through the impermanence of the art. Sometimes it's hard for me to believe, but every one of the altars I've ever made with

LAST, A WORD TO YOUR FIVE-YEAR-OLD SELF:

The world outside,
she's calling you.
Crack the door and
leave your home.

Become the explorer
you were meant to be.
And voyage all over the wilds
that was once your neighborhood.

For there you'll find the treasure
hidden under your feet.
And with the flicker of your imagination
everything can be anything.

Spotted feathers and fuzzy leaves
become the map of a whole universe.
Flower bursts and electric bark
arrange a symphony on the ground.

Life becomes so alive again
and so do you.

So take the hand
of that adult of yours.
Lead them back out.

Out of their figure-outy minds,
out of their never-ending scrolling screens,
out of their worries and woes and long list
of to-dos,
and into belonging.

To this timeless story,
to this changing world,
to their deep and nourishing creative well
that they have always been a part of
and had access to.

This greater story is called by many names
but can be experienced as
Wonder
Delight
or even just
Happiness.

my hands, thousands of hours spent in fierce concentration and wild imagination, no longer exists. Ephemerality and impermanence have always been the greatest and richest teaching of this art, and they remind us that life is forever changing and fleeting and invaluably precious.

What we have is only here right now, and this moment yearns for the fullness of our presence and attention lest we take it for granted. While every altar I have ever made is an expression of my love of life, their decay makes that love overflow even more.

Inspiration:
ALTARS FROM AROUND THE WORLD

Let us build altars to the beautiful necessity, which secures that all is made of one piece.

—*Ralph Waldo Emerson*

My son, Zakai and I have been making altars together at least once a week. Together, we are paying closer attention to the dynamic life force that is always changing all around us.

—*Reva and Zakai Nevah in Sebastopol, California*

It began very simply; someone else had arranged a few pinecones and sticks. I added some leaves, spaced it out, and cleaned it up a bit. I came back a day later and it had even more intricacies. I added even more. We were communicating silently through art. I still have no idea who my fellow collaborators were. I'm so thankful for this group art piece that we made while on our moments of contemplative walking.

—*Morgan Klein in Cobb, California*

I recently lost my younger brother to a drug overdose and was feeling overwhelmed with grief and emotions. So I sat and started to create. I must have been there for three hours or more, I don't even know! Time flew by and I became obsessed. I love this practice, I love what it has given me. It has brought much peace to my life. This altar is in memory of my brother.

—*Billi Jo Murphy in Bay Head, New Jersey*

A few years ago, my older sister passed away from a long illness. I made this mandala (shells, rocks, and little daisies) in her honor while visiting a beach in Ballycotton, Ireland. She loved the ocean, and we would often visit it together when I still lived in Santa Cruz. I miss my family and hometown, and connecting with nature this way is so healing. It brings them and me beauty and joy.

—*Desirée Fernandez in Ballycotton, Ireland*

I commute into Boston, working at a fast-paced technology company. During lunchtime, I make it a priority to get outside! I discovered a nearby park and running trails near my office. So I go . . . making lunchtime altars. There is something so liberating about doing this in the middle of the workday. It shifts my perspective. Getting outdoors (even on the coldest of days), experiencing solitude and stillness, and being creative—totally ignites my soul.

—*Sara Lehmer, Boston, MA*

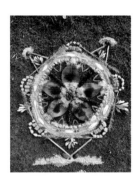

This mandala , as it was forming, reminded me of the strong family cultures of the Pacific nations. Earthy, big-hearted, and calm people. I used materials from the edges of the beach: sand, cuttlefish, pandanus, grasses, fig leaves, succulents, and pumice from volcanoes that floated from maybe Indonesia? It was so nice to leave knowing the mandala was there for other members of my hometown community to enjoy and interpret in the way they wanted to.

—*Melissa Hellwig in Australia*

I crafted the altar in this picture while I was romping around the Carpathian Mountains, where, before the Holocaust, there were hundreds of thriving Jewish communities: the classic, old, rural shtetls. As I walked, the spruce cones and the wildflowers were calling to me. I began gathering . . . then building. This was for Mother Earth, for the land that held my ancestors. This was a way to express and process beyond the limitations of words. I felt lighter as I parted ways with the altar, like something had been processed and released.

—*Daniel Berchenko in Ukraine*

With care, I had foraged from beds of shale and other organic materials unique to the land. I tended daily to the finished altar, rearranging the shifted pieces and bringing it fresh wildflowers for the weekend. This piece was so alive: little bugs constantly hovered over it. The stream gushed by a few feet away. By the last day, green shoots had started regrowing within the circle . . . no creative medium feels as magical to me as working with the Earth herself.

—*Sarah Bista in Stephentown, New York*

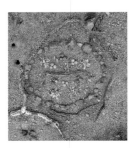

I made this circular altar on January 20, 2017, just off a trail in the Tucson Mountains, as a prayer for peace and safety for all during the Women's March taking place the next day. . . I gathered native sandstone pebbles, brittlebush tips, jojoba, cholla fruits, and cholla bones for this mandala. A year later I visited the spot and searched for this altar but didn't find it. Possibly the stones had been scattered by animals, but a cairn I had built the same day as the circle, farther up the trail, remained.

—*Kirsten Bosnak in Tucson Mountains, Arizona*

II decided to make an altar to honor Monty, my recently deceased cat. It was made up of 19 concentric circles, one for each year of his life. I knew it ultimately wouldn't be a permanent art piece, but I wanted it to stay intact at least until I finished it, and so I chose objects I hoped would not easily blow away. It took four days, working on it two to three hours each day, to complete. I had not expected how healing the experience of creating the mandala was for me. It became a way and a place to channel my sadness.

—*Theresa Smith Murray in North Yarmouth, Maine*

This piece came about as I was walking down to the "crik" behind my house in Galloway, Ohio. I noticed some fresh icicles hanging from my barn along the way. I carefully plucked each one at the base, being careful not to break or drop them. I started placing them, by size, strategically around a circle on the ice, smoothed out with a warm hand to form the shape of a clock. I did not use numbers or hands on this particular clock, though I was reminded of a now-vintage wall clock that hung on one of my aunt's walls when I was a child in the 1970s. I wanted this clock to simply designate the time as "Winter Time."

—*Bill Dawson in Galloway, Ohio*

After collecting mussel shells from the beach for several days, I began laying them out in a mandala form. I "goofed" and did not notice how close I was from the water's edge or if the tide was going out or coming in. Midway through laying out the mandala I became hyperaware that the water was rapidly moving toward me. It seemed that the water and I were playing some kind of game . . . not only was I playing with nature, but nature was playing with me. It made me happy.

—*Gloria Lamson in southeast Alaska*

I made this with flowers and seeds I collected from our rambla . . . I made this for my mum and dad on our old doorstep . . . because I love Morning Altars and I always share your photos with my mum.

—*Arabella Kelly in southern Spain*

I made this altar a week after my beloved Uncle Martin passed away from cancer. I set some time aside for myself one warm afternoon and gathered all the materials from my yard: chestnuts, chestnut shells, hawthorn berry, walnut shells, nandina leaves, and calendula. The most powerful part of the process for me was gifting myself the time to make this altar. It was like I was carving out a little bit of time and space for my grief, a safe space where I could just sit and feel it. What emerged out of that time and space was a tribute not only to my uncle but also a way to honor myself and the passage of the time that we spent together in this lifetime. Within hours, squirrels and birds dismantled the altar, reminding me of how natural it is for life to dissolve into new forms, and that each death brings with it the potential for something new to be born.

—*Karina Towers in Portland, Oregon*

I went out onto the land to find balance. My ceremony would consist of building a circle, representing my life, and moving things in and out of it, until the balance felt right. I began to collect what came to me: long brown pine needles, a few pinecones, moss, some leaves, and dried cedar twigs. Finding a spot on a path on a small hill, I built the altar. As I did so, a new understanding came.

—*Sharon Reinbott in Berkeley, California*

Acknowledgments:
ALTARS OF GRATITUDE

It's truly an odd and mysterious thing to be an impermanent earth artist in the 21st century. It's not necessarily a career that your parents dream you'll pursue when you grow up. But maybe this dream is far older than them? Maybe someone long ago, an ancestor long forgotten, envisioned a time such as this when there would come a real need to wonder again. Maybe that old-timer foresaw an era and place so disconnected from the living world, so entranced with speed and distraction, so addicted to certainty and information, that they planted a seed that wasn't meant to sprout until now.

At the best of times, I truly don't understand how my life's path led me here. But maybe this path wasn't mine to choose in the first place. Maybe I'm just fulfilling an older dream so that generations of people I will never meet and a time that I will never see may have a way of dreaming with the Earth again.

To sit at the helm of such a dream cannot be accomplished alone. For both art and Earth teach us that we are never separate but are interwoven always with each other and all of life, even if we forget this at times. The art and altars in this book are all made from many separate pieces that when they come together make something uniquely beauty. This is exactly the way Morning Altars has been born as well. For all those hands, hearts, and wild unbound imaginations that have gathered around this small and fleeting enterprise, I lay altars of thanks at your feet so that you may know that this beauty is your beauty.

An altar of praise & pinecones laid down to that ragged caravan of Orphan Wisdom Scholars, a motley crew of those willing to carry the burdensome privilege of learning unauthorized things in a troubled time with knee-buckling eloquence and style; and specifically to Matthew Stillman, Ryan DeMatteo, Annie Levin, Raven Miller, Tyla Fae, Rebecca Roveto, Steven and Sarah Marshank, Holly Pruett, Chantal Gagnon, Tad Hargrave, Ian MacKenzie, Elin Agla, Natasha Kong, and all the unnamed but needed others.

An altar of love & cedar arranged for that wild community of Wilderness Jews in California, New York, and across the globe, who gather together to redeem and revive our ancient traditions as Earth traditions; and of course to my beloveds Tali Weinberg, Simcha Schwartz, Kait Singley, Yigal Deutscher, Zelig Golden, Rachel Ruach, Caitlin Sislin, Heather AfterFive, Julie Wolk, Lauren Brown, Rachel Rose Reid, Earnest Sophie Vener, Leah Lamb, Rae Abileah, Jen Myzel, Zivar Amrami, Zach Friedman, Shoshanna Jedwab, and Rabbi Jill Hammer. Our ancestors are smiling with us.

An altar of thanks & milk thistle offered to those faithful midwives and doulas who gathered around the birthing of this book and whose guidance and support won't be easily forgotten; specifically the gentle and strong hands of editors Kristy Lin Billuni and Anton Dudley; the brilliant photographer, Brooke Porter; the foreseeing council of my agent, Katherine Latshaw of Folio Literary Management; the upright dedication of my excellent publisher, Ann Treistman; and all the magicians at The Countryman Press and W. W. Norton.

An altar of hymns & sagebrush built to that dusty, rowdy cavalcade from Boulder Mountain, Utah, and specifically to Ron Johnson and Brandie Hardman of its Guest Ranch, whose vision and generosity gave this writing a majestic place to be born; to Malcom Love, Arnie, Colyer Hoyt, Brad and Amy Anderson, Leilani and Sylas Navar, Scott Brodie, Eric Arballo, and Stevo Comeau, and to Trevor Oswalt of East Forest, my steadfast ally and brother from numerous life times.

An altar of bows & branches assembled to all those who stand tall as the godparents of this endeavor and to whom Morning Altars has become something worth standing for; including the divine HeatherAsh Amara, the stout and generous Mike Carnohan, the swarthy Thomas Brodahl, and my fierce and dedicated wrangler, Shoshanna Howard for your friendship, management, and persistent belief that Morning Altars is needed in this world.

An altar of tribute & trumpet flowers gathered to those whose vision included seeing a large-scale Morning Altar sit at the heart of their festivals and conferences; specifically to Marisa Weppner of Treefort Music Festival, Peter Sabbeth and the Andy Warhol Preserve, and Jennie Witt and all those angels from the Wanderlust Festival.

An altar of reverence & rose buds composed to those sapient storytellers and elders, gifts to these uncertain times, who have entrusted me with a great remembering of how it has been and how it could be otherwise; kissing the hands and feet of the beloved Stephen Jenkinson, Nathalie Roy, Clyde Hall, Jon Young, and Joanna Macy.

An altar of kisses & seashells created to those of my bone and blood, living and dead whose existence underwrites my existence; always to my mother and father, Wendy and Michael, my mercurial brother Matthew and his partner Kaci, and my grandmother Shirley who reminds me every day not to take it all so seriously. And to those who have become family over all these years, including Lilli Weisz, Jordanna Dworkin and Behnam Vadi, Lela Davia, whom I have had the privilege of sharing this land with, and all the teens, past, present, and future of my weekly Fire Circle at Rodef Sholom.

An altar of appreciation & acorns constructed to my communities on Instagram and Facebook, thousands of people I may never meet but who continue to gather around this art and whose comments, photos, emojis, and inspiration feed me the strength to continue bringing beauty to this world, including all the altar makers who have contributed their art and stories to this book so others would be inspired to make their own. Your support nourishes my roots.

And an altar of hallelujah & honeysuckles made to all those many, many places that invited me to roam their bodies, touch their grounds, adorn their faces, and who claim me as their own; and especially to Wildcat Canyon, California, Boulder Mountain, Utah, and New York, New York. May the people learn to remember and honor their relationship with you and, consequently, themselves.

REFERENCES

Berry, Thomas. *The Great Work: Our Way into the Future*. New York: Bell Tower, 1999.

Bogart, Anne. *What's the Story: Essays about Art, Theatre and Storytelling*. Abingdon, UK: Routledge, 2014.

Chödrön, Pema. *The Places that Scare You: A Guide to Fearlessness in Difficult Times*. Boulder, CO: Shambhala Publications, 2002.

Conrad, Joseph. *The Nigger of the 'Narcissus' and Other Stories*. New York: Penguin Classics, 2007.

De Mille, Agnes. *Martha: The Life and Work of Martha Graham*. New York: Random House, 1991.

De Saint-Exupéry, Antoine. *The Little Prince*. Willmington, DE: Mariner Books, 2000.

Deutscher, Yigal. *Envisioning Sabbatical Culture: A Shmita Manifesto*. 7Seeds. Retrieved from http://7seedsproject.org/manifesto/

DiDonato, Joyce. Medici.tv. Video file. (October 26, 2017.) Retrieved from www.facebook.com/medicitv/videos/10154767153917352/?hc_ref=ARQcHGOQwppFTKwqIhmmOZiPTNuG4MUu391v68pw1zRKA3TDo-6K7CJkHnE24wJDHdA&pnref=story

Eisenstein, Charles. *Sacred Economics: Money, Gift, and Society in the Age of Transition*. Berkeley, CA: North Atlantic Books, 2011.

Emerson, Ralph Waldo. *The Major Prose*. Boston: Belknap Press, 2015.

Farley, Morgan. *Clearing*. Gratefulness. Retrieved from https://gratefulness.org/resource/clearing/

Gibran, Kahlil. *The Prophet*. New York: Alfred A. Knopf, 1923.

Goldsworthy, Andy. "Sculptor Turns Rain, Ice and Trees Into 'Ephemeral Works,'" radio interview by Terry Gross, NPR.org/2015/(October 8, 2015.) Retrieved from https://www.npr.10/08/446731282/sculptor-turns-rain-ice-and-trees-into-ephemeral-works

Govinda, Anagarika. *The Way of White Clouds: A Buddhist Pilgrim in Tibet*. Boulder, CO: Shambhala. Reprint edition, 1988.

Hanh, Thich Nhat. *The Heart of the Buddha's Teaching: Transforming Suffering into Peace, Joy, and Liberation*. New York: Broadway Books, 1999.

Heschel, Abraham Joshua. "Radical Amazement." Retrieved from https://www.youtube.com/watch?v=FEXK9xcRCho

Hyde, Lewis. *The Gift: Creativity and the Artist in the Modern World*. New York: Vintage Books, 1979.

Jenkinson, Stephen. *Die Wise: A Manifesto for Sanity and Soul*. Berkeley, CA: North Atlantic Books, 2015.

Kimmerer, Robin Wall. *Braiding Sweetgrass: Indigenous Wisdom, Scientific Knowledge, and the Teaching of Plants*. Minneapolis, MN: Milkweed Editions, 2013.

Louv, Richard. *Last Child in the Woods: Saving Our Children from Nature-Deficit Disorder*. Chapel Hill, NC: Algonquin Books, 2006.

Macfarlane, Robert. *Landmarks*. London: Hamish Hamilton, 2015.

Machado, Antonio. *Times Alone: Selected Poems of Antonio Machado*. Middleton, CT: Wesleyan Poetry in Translation, 1983.

Meade, Michael. *Living Myth: Serving the Dream of the World*, Episode 38. Audio podcast (September 28, 2017). Retrieved from http://mosaicvoices.org/podcast-archives.html

O'Donohue, John. *Longing and Belonging*. Audiobook. Louisville, CO: Sounds True.

Oliver, Mary. *American Primitive*. Boston: Back Bay Books, 1983.

——. *Evidence: Poems*. Boston: Beacon Press. Reprint edition, 2010.

——. *Wild Geese*. Northumberland, UK: Bloodaxe World Poets, 2004.

Plotkin, Bill. *Nature and the Human Soul: Cultivating Wholeness and Community in a Fragmented World*. Novato, CA: New World Library, 2008.

Pope, Alexander. *Selected Poetry*. UK: Oxford World's Classics, 2008.

Popova, Maria. *Poetry and the Revolution of Being: Jane Hirshfield on*

How Great Art Transforms Us. Brain Pickings. Retrieved from: https://www.brainpickings.org/2017/10/02/jane-hirshfield-ten-windows-poetry/

Prechtel, Martín. *The Disobedience of the Daughter of the Sun*. Berkeley, CA: North Atlantic Books, 2005.

Prechtel, Martín. *The Smell of Rain on Dust: Grief and Praise*. Berkeley, CA: North Atlantic Books, 2015.

Proust, Marcel. *In Search of Lost Time*. London: Centaur Classics, 2017.

Rilke, Rainer Maria. Excerpted from *Letters to a Young Poet*. The Sun Magazine. Retrieved from https://www.thesunmagazine.org/issues/420/from-letters-to-a-young-poet

Rumi, Jalal al-Din. *The Essential Rumi* (Coleman Barks, Trans.). New York: HarperCollins, 1996.

Schneider, Michael S. *A Beginner's Guide to Constructing the Universe: The Mathematical Archetypes of Nature, Art, and Science*. New York: HarperCollins. Kindle Edition.

Shaw, Martin. *Scatterlings: An Interview with English Storyteller Martin Shaw on Nomads, Being Local and Belonging*. Audio Interview. Retrieved from http://marketingforhippies.com/scatterlings/

——. *Scatterlings: Getting Claimed in the Age of Amnesia*. Ashland, OR: White Cloud Press, 2016.

Simone, Nina. *Nina Simone: Great Performances—Live College Concerts & Interview*. Movie. Retrieved from https://www.youtube.com/watch?v=0qL3nHvliN4

Swimme, Brian. *Earth's Imagination*. Episode 4. Class lecture.

Tharp, Twyla. *The Creative Habit: Learn It and Use It for Life*. New York: Simon & Schuster, 2003.

Tolkien, J. R. R. *The Lord of the Rings*. London: HarperCollins, 1994.

Turner, Toko-pa. *Belonging: Remembering Ourselves Home*. Salt Spring Island, BC: Her Own Room Press, 2017.

Trevino, Haven. *The Tao of Healing: Meditations for Body and Spirit*. Novato, CA: New World Library, 1993.

Wagoner, David. *Collected Poems, 1956–76*. Bloomington, IN: Indiana University Press, 1976.

Waheed, Nayyirah. s*alt*. CreateSpace Independent Publishing Platform, 2013.

Weller, Francis. "The Geography of Sorrow: Francis Weller on Navigating Our Losses," interview by Tim McKee, *The Sun*, issue 478 (October 2015).

Whitman, Walt. *The Complete Poems of Walt Whitman*. Hertfordshire, UK: Wordsworth Editions, 1998.

Whyte, David. *Consolations: The Solace, Nourishment and Underlying Meaning of Everyday Words*. Langley, WA: Many Rivers Press, 2015.

——. *Everything Is Waiting for You*. Langley, WA: Many Rivers Press, 2003.

Wilde, Oscar. *The Decay of Lying and Other Essays*. London: Penguin Classics, 2010.

DAY SCHILDKRET is an earth artist, educator, and public speaker who teaches workshops internationally for communities, festivals, and corporations, as well as mentoring individuals in their creative life purpose. His work, which focuses on why creative living, beauty making, and impermanence are needed now more than ever, has been featured in *Vice*, *Buzzfeed*, *Well + Good*, *Spirituality & Health*, and elsewhere. He lives in California's Bay Area. For more information, please see www.morningaltars.com.

CREDITS
Pages 4, 8, 22, 24, 35, 78, 132, 152 (bottom), 168, 170, 190, 216, 222, 229, 234: Brooke Porter

Page 27: Ian MacKenzie; page 230: Reva Nevah (top left), Morgan Klein (center left), Billi Jo Murphy (bottom left), Desirée Fernandez (right); page 231: Sara Lehmer (top left), Melissa Hellwig (center left), Anthony Gomes IV Photography @AGIVphotography (bottom), Daniel Berchenko (right); page 232: Kirsten Bosnak (Lawrence, Kansas) (top left), Bill Dawson @earth_art_bill (bottom left), Theresa Smith Murray (top right), Gloria Lamson (bottom right); page 233: Karina Towers (left), Arabella B. Kelly (top right), Sharon Reinbott (bottom right); page 236: Julia Maryanska.

Page 39: Lines from "Lost" in *Traveling Light: Collected and New Poems*. Copyright 1999 by David Wagoner. Used with permission of the University of Illinois Press.

Page 67: Rumi translation © Coleman Barks.

For information about permission to reproduce selections from this book, write to Permissions, The Countryman Press, 500 Fifth Avenue, New York, NY 10110

For information about special discounts for bulk purchases, please contact W. W. Norton Special Sales at specialsales@wwnorton.com or 800-233-4830

Manufacturing by ToppanLeefung
Book design by Anna Reich
Production manager: Devon Zahn

The Countryman Press
www.countrymanpress.com

A division of W. W. Norton & Company, Inc.
500 Fifth Avenue, New York, NY 10110
www.wwnorton.com

978-1-68268-251-7

10   9   8   7   6   5   4   3   2   1